HERE IS WHAT REVIEWERS AND READERS ARE SAYING ABOUT *PET SITTING FOR PROFIT:*

"This book is an absolute must. It covers everything from office procedures, legal structure, telephone techniques and customer complaints to contracts and advertising."
Dog Week

"We highly recommend this . . . a must for anybody interested in taking up pet sitting as a business or as a sideline."
Cats magazine

"Moran deals with the basics of starting your own pet sitting business. The book covers all aspects of starting a home-based business."
Aiken Standard (South Carolina)

" 'Good things come in small packages' will be proven for those who read Patti Moran's timely treatise: Pet Sitting for Profit. . . . *The book holds an opportunity for all pet lovers, for those who wish to be their own boss on a full time basis, those who want or need the income of a second job, as well as those retired and desirous of meaningful activity."*
The Latham Letter

"Running a pet sitting business is more complicated than it sounds, and Moran provides a wealth of detail about how the business should be handled. . . . The book is certainly a handy guide for anyone considering such a business, but it also contains helpful information for people who need pet-sitters."
Cat Fancy

"Includes everything you need to know about setting up the business."
Rainbo Electronic Reviews

"The book is great. It certainly will take all the guesswork out of setting up a pet sitting business!"
Elizabeth Nicholson
Richton Park, Illinois

Pet Sitting
for
Profit

A COMPLETE MANUAL FOR PROFESSIONAL SUCCESS

Patti J. Moran

HOWELL BOOK HOUSE

New York

Maxwell Macmillan Canada
Toronto

Maxwell Macmillan International
New York   Oxford   Singapore   Sydney

Howell Book House
Macmillan Publishing Company
866 Third Avenue
New York, NY 10022

Maxwell Macmillan Canada, Inc.
1200 Eglinton Avenue East
Suite 200
Don Mills, Ontario M3C 3N1

Macmillan Publishing Company is part of the Maxwell Communication Group of Companies.

Library of Congress Cataloging-in-Publication Data

Moran, Patti J.
    Pet sitting for profit: a complete manual for professional success / by Patti
J. Moran.
        p.   cm.
    ISBN 0-87605-770-9
    1. Pet sitting—Handbooks, manuals, etc.   I. Title.
SF414.34.M67   1991
636.088′7—dc20   91-15959
                                                                                      CIP

Macmillan books are available at special discounts for bulk purchases for sales promotions, premiums, fund-raising, or educational use. For details, contact:

                        Special Sales Director
                        Macmillan Publishing Company
                        866 Third Avenue
                        New York, NY 10022

10 9 8 7 6 5 4

First Howell Book House edition 1991

Printed in the United States of America

*For my three angels, Lonnie, Lucy and Ennis.
And, of course, for Mike, whose love and
support make it all possible.*

Contents

Introduction

No one knows what he can do till he tries.

Publilius Syrus, *Maxim 786*

If at once you have begun, never leave it till it's done.
Be it big or be it small, do it well or not at all.

my mother

WHEN I PAUSE to reflect upon the last eight years, it's almost overwhelming to consider the changes and growth the pet sitting field has experienced, and how pet sitting affected me personally and professionally. Little did I know in 1983 that my opening a small, part-time pet-sitting service would lead me not only to author this book, but to serve as a national spokesperson for our thriving, new service industry. There's a phrase that describes our progress perfectly: Pet sitters have truly come a long way.

Today's new pet sitter has so much more information available which, if used to advantage, will greatly increase the likelihood that his or her pet-sitting business will be a successful endeavor. There is now a national trade organization for pet sitters, quality time-saving products for pet-sitting professionals and this book detailing all my experience.

A friend recently asked why I was spending so much time revising and expanding this book when the preceding editions have sold so well. Several reasons immediately came to mind.

First of all, in anything I do, I like to do it well (thanks in large part to my dear, late mother, who is quoted above). This philosophy was evident in the first editions of *Pet Sitting for Profit*, and I believe my thoroughness is what has earned my book its reputation as the "bible of pet sitting." With such high praise from thousands of readers, I unknowingly created equally high expectations for subsequent editions!

Secondly, there have been changes in the pet-sitting industry since the book was first published, and these now need to be addressed. For example, the critical need for good (but often difficult to obtain) business insurance was stressed in earlier editions. With the proliferation of pet sitters in recent years this need has been recognized as a standard for the industry, and the insurance has become much easier to find. Now, however, there's a new emphasis on protecting the name of your business. When there were only a handful of sitters, name recognition and protection weren't given a second thought. Now, with our industry growing so rapidly, this is an area that requires careful consideration.

My third reason for devoting so much time to this new edition is the simple fact that I continue to learn about pet sitting. Unlike other professions that require a particular course of study or that are well established, pet sitting is an evolving field. After all, in the business of pet sitting, no two days are alike. Each customer, pet and home has the potential to offer a novel situation or problem. In a few cases, new knowledge has caused me to change my mind about something I wrote earlier. Therefore, I must humbly and honestly tell you that I do not profess to know it all—though I do have more experience than most in this field. I think it's the variety and ongoing learning process that keeps this career so interesting and appealing to me.

A final motivation has come from you, the reader. Many of you have written to ask me questions, solicit advice or share your own experiences in starting and operating your pet-sitting businesses. While I've not been able to reply personally in all cases, I have read and appreciated your communication. It's through your correspondence that I've noted mutual concerns and areas needing more attention in revised versions of *Pet Sitting for Profit*. I thank you for letting me know how I can improve this book and better help the pet sitters of tomorrow. I sincerely hope this new edition meets the high standards you've come to expect from me.

Many readers have been curious about my background, how I came up with the idea of pet sitting and how I came to write a book about the subject. So, for those who are interested in such things, I offer the following.

It all started in 1983 when I was laid off from my job. If anyone had told me then that losing my job was a blessing in disguise, I wouldn't have believed them. I had been hired by a large manufacturing company one week after graduating from college. I spent seven years there in employee relations, working my way up from a clerical position to management. My position was stress-filled due to the workload and company politics. The salary and benefits, however, were generous and, somehow, I resigned myself to the fact that it was easier to stay than to leave. Then, when the company experienced a severe downturn in business, almost half of the employees, including me, found themselves without a job.

Since I needed the income, I found myself exploring job options. The idea of having my own business had always appealed to me and, at that point, it was more attractive than ever. The thought of not having to answer to anyone else or depend upon anyone else for job security encouraged me to seriously consider starting my own business. My biggest question was what kind of business to open.

As I slowly researched various ideas, I also took time out for myself. I planted a garden. I took classes. I mowed the grass on cool mornings. I shopped during the day when there was hardly anyone in the stores. These activities were all luxuries to me after seven years in the corporate rat race, years when time was limited and dictated by the demands of my job. I rapidly became spoiled by my flexible schedule, and the idea of an eight-to-five office job actually grew abhorrent. What could I do that would provide adequate income and also allow me time to enjoy this new-found and treasured lifestyle?

The answer came when a good friend who'd recently moved to another city visited for a weekend. Knowing how crazy she was about her dog, I inquired about what type of arrangements she had made for her pet's care during her absence. She told me she had hired a pet sitter to come to her house twice a day. Little did I know then that this innocent question and her answer would change my life as I knew it . . . but it was then and there that the light bulb went on in my head. I was immediately intrigued.

Having three dogs and a cat of my own, I was all too familiar with the problems a pet owner faces when traveling. I knew firsthand that the option of a pet-sitting service would be a needed and welcome one in our community. Furthermore, pet sitting could be done in just a few hours in the morning or in the afternoon, so I'd have some flexibility and extra hours in my day for other activities. It wouldn't require a costly inventory, and I certainly wouldn't need an expensive wardrobe. I also didn't see any need for renting office space; pet sitting seemed to me to be an ideal choice for a home business. And since I loved animals, pet sitting would allow me to get paid for doing something I enjoyed. It quickly became apparent to me that a pet-sitting business had many advantages and incorporated all the things I was looking for in a new career venture. Although it was scary to consider the risk I'd be taking in opening an "unheard of" business in our town, I felt I'd be crazy not to at least give it a try.

As I made preparations to open my pet-sitting business, there were times when I thought maybe I was crazy. First of all, although there was a lot of information available about how to start a small business, I couldn't find any information that specifically addressed pet sitting. Secondly, I was often not taken seriously when I told people what I was attempting to do. Some of my friends just couldn't believe I planned to "baby-sit for pets and clean litter boxes for a living." And, as I searched for insurance coverage, many doors were shut in my face.

But, as the saying goes, where there's a will, there's a way. In late 1983, my pet-sitting service opened for business. And since that time, this relatively new and innovative business has provided me with a very rewarding, interesting and profitable career.

I was originally prompted to write this book for a couple of reasons. As people in other parts of the country heard about my business, I began receiving requests for help and information from budding entrepreneurs who wanted to start such a business in their own area. Since there was nothing available in writing to help me when I first started pet sitting, I knew firsthand the need for such guidance. I also wrote the book (and initially published it myself) because I believed that pet sitting is a viable new profession. It provides a valuable service for pets and their owners and an enjoyable and profitable way for pet lovers to earn a livelihood.

Although I've seen pet sitting grow from only a few of us back in 1983 to an estimated 350 companies in the United States today, I believe that this field is still in its infancy. The increased demand for and credibility of pet sitting make it a good career opportunity. I like to think that I've played an important role in bringing this profession the respectability and attention that it deserves. As such, I have an investment to protect and have set forth my hard-won knowledge in this book to professionally guide others interested in pursuing this career.

There is a lot more to pet sitting than meets the eye, and it's not, as some would think, a fast way to make a buck. Hanging a shingle out and calling yourself a pet sitter is not enough to be successful in today's business world. Even worse, it reflects poorly upon our industry. I urge you, as a prospective entrepreneur, to give this promising and unique venture your careful consideration. Conscientious forethought will assure that your journey into pet sitting will be a successful and satisfying adventure.

Pet Sitting
for
Profit

1

The Concept of
Pet Sitting

THE CONCEPT of pet sitting is relatively new and, while the industry is growing rapidly, the idea is still somewhat foreign to many people. Since many animal lovers have never heard of this service, they have never considered pet sitting as a profitable business venture. But this is changing as people hear about personalized in-home pet care and recognize the potential a pet-sitting business can hold—potential for self-employment, for providing a needed community service, for creating the lifestyle you've always dreamed of, and for significant profits.

By becoming a pet sitter, you'll enter the service industry, which is expected to be a powerful economic force of the future. Experts say that people today need services of all sorts. Statistics show that in the United States:

- Services now account for nearly 70% of the Gross National Product.
- Twenty-two million of the 25 million jobs created since 1970 were in the service sector.

• Nine out of ten jobs created between now and 1995 are expected to be in the service industry.

These figures are very encouraging to anyone thinking of starting a pet-sitting service. With such a business, you'll join the fast track of the new American economy.

There are trends in today's society that have made service businesses a fast-growing industry. Two-income families have become the norm, making services both necessary and affordable to these families. Young professionals are delaying marriage and/or children and many own pets and take better care of them than ever before. And with an estimated 56 million cats, 52 million dogs, 45 million birds and 250 million fish in the United States, there is a definite market for pet sitting. These figures don't include the other household pets such as ferrets, rabbits, gerbils, hamsters, guinea pigs, turtles, frogs and snakes that require care and attention.

Another trend in American society is the move toward self-employment, often in a home-based business. More and more of us are discovering that our jobs rule our lives and that, contrary to generations past, there is no such thing as job security within a company in today's world. Self-employment allows you to take more control over your life, your career, your schedule, your income. As a pet sitter, you are your own boss. You decide when you work, where you work, what you charge and for whom you work. There is no one looking over your shoulder, and no time clock to punch.

There is independence and pride in being your own boss. Being the owner of such a business will give you an increased sense of self-worth and confidence in your abilities. The satisfaction you'll derive is only one of the many benefits you'll experience. And although you may choose to work longer hours, work is usually more enjoyable when you're working for yourself.

Being a pet sitter gives you flexibility with your daily schedule. You'll no longer be bound by a rigid framework of set hours. Since most pet-sitting visits are made during the early morning or early evening, you'll probably have the largest part of the day free to pursue other interests or even to work another job if you wish. The flexible working hours make pet sitting an ideal part-time business or source of second income as this work can be adapted around most schedules. And, of course, it can be operated as a full-time business in many cities.

YOUR OWN POTENTIAL

Becoming a pet sitter will definitely provide a reliable means of income. Whether you sit independently or employ a staff of sitters, there is money to be made by providing this valuable service to your community. The amount of income you can expect to make will depend on several variables. The location of a pet-sitting service is a factor. A heavily populated city area naturally will provide a greater number of customers than a rural-based setting. A part-time sitting service will not generate as much income as a full-time service. And a pet sitter working alone will not generate as much revenue as a staff of pet sitters.

Another important ingredient to the income potential of a pet-sitting service is the personality of the owner. If you do nothing but print up some business cards and sit by the phone, you will find yourself only dreaming of income. If you commit yourself to the success of your business and then actively and aggressively pursue this commitment, your potential for higher income is considerably improved. Although pet sitting is a terrific business idea, it takes more than a good idea to make a business a success. I'm often asked by readers ''How much can I expect to make?'' and this is one question that I'm afraid I can't answer. Your capabilities, desires and level of commitment will determine how great your return will be. I can tell you that pet sitting has been profitable for me, and I can provide you with information and tools that will point you in a successful direction.

WHAT IS NEEDED

Unlike many other business opportunities, pet sitting involves limited start-up costs. As of this writing (and depending upon the cost of living in various parts of the country), I estimate that a pet-sitting business can be opened with a $3,000–$5,000 investment. Although you can spend much more, it's really not necessary. After all, there is no costly inventory required, so your primary expenses will be for office equipment, supplies and professional services. And many people can work out of their homes, saving rent for office space. The details of how to open a pet-sitting service economically will be discussed later.

Pet sitting requires very little in the way of past experience or expertise. There is no specific educational program necessary, but any background in working with or caring for pets will be a plus. In addition, any prior business courses or business experience is bound to be helpful in your operation. The most important prerequisite of a pet sitter is that he or she needs to be a pet lover. Other than this, possessing good common sense and a sense of humor is essential for making a success of pet sitting.

Work becomes fun! Many sitters have said to me that pet sitting is so enjoyable they almost feel as if they aren't working. Each pet, home and customer is different, adding variety and interest to the job. Pets and their owners are appreciative of your efforts, and the pets readily let you know it. Perhaps you have worked for that boss or supervisor whose praise, compliments or positive ''strokes'' were few and far between—not so with pet sitting. That wagging tail or contented purring lets you know someone is glad you're there. And

furthermore, pets don't care what you're wearing or how you look. It's a wonderful feeling to wake up on a rainy morning, throw on jeans and a sweatshirt and head out the door to places where you'll be eagerly and warmly greeted.

You'll also take pride in knowing you're providing such a valuable service to your community. Pet owners have had few choices in the past. Traditionally, they could either leave their pets in unfamiliar environments, impose upon a friend or neighbor, or stay at home. By opening a pet-sitting service, you provide an attractive alternative for pet owners, enabling them to travel assured that their pets and homes are in good hands.

THE ALTERNATIVES TO PET SITTING

Let's discuss the choices a pet owner has had in the past and why personalized home pet care is the best alternative.

When faced with traveling, a pet owner has usually called upon a kennel or veterinarian to board a pet. And many pet owners have had a trip or vacation spoiled by the memory of those sad and confused eyes of the pet they left behind. They worry about the welfare of their animals. I know of a few pets who even have to be tranquilized when boarded at a kennel. And many older pets are traumatized by a change in environment. With a pet sitter, the owner can leave the pet in its own secure, familiar space. Like people, pets are creatures of habit, and by staying in their own home they are able to follow their normal eating, medication and exercise routines. Such familiarity contributes to the happiness and health-iness of the pet.

When using a pet sitter, the owner is not inconvenienced by having to transport his or her pet to the vet or kennel, and the pet avoids the trauma of such a trip. An additional benefit of staying at home is that the likelihood of exposure to illnesses is greatly reduced for the pet. And perhaps most important, a pet receives loving, individual attention from its personal pet sitter.

Another common option many pet owners use is having a friend or neighborhood youngster care for their pets. In today's transient society, many people don't know their neighbors well enough to feel comfortable in making this request, or they just don't want to impose. What if the young person proves unreliable? What if something should happen and the pet becomes ill, or something in the house gets broken? Such circumstances could certainly strain or ruin a friendship or neighbor relations. There is security in calling a professionally operated pet-sitting service employing sitters accustomed, for example, to transporting sick pets to the vet. (A service may also be insured for breakage in a customer's home.) A pet-sitting service has reliable, mature, trustworthy individuals who enjoy the business of caring for pets. A pet sitter can be counted on to treat each pet and home as if it were his or her own.

There are additional benefits to the pet owner when engaging the services of a sitter. A pet sitter keeps an eye on each home by doing such things as bringing in the mail and newspapers, alternating lights, opening and closing curtains or blinds, and watering house plants. These small services give a home a lived-in look while the owner is away. Such crime-deterrent measures result in peace of mind for the absent homeowner. It is a pleasure for returning homeowners to find healthy, happy pets awaiting their arrival—and their home as they left it.

Expense may be the only negative for a pet owner who hires a sitter. A pet sitter is usually a bit more expensive than a boarding kennel or obliging neighbor. But the number of repeat clients I have, and the feedback I get from them, attests to the fact that most pet owners think the convenience and advantages are well worth the extra expense.

THE NEED IS EVERYWHERE

One of the most positive factors to consider when evaluating pet sitting as a possible business is that virtually every community, both urban and rural, really needs such a service. Where there are people, there are pets. Recent research has identified the therapeutic effect that pets have on people. Pets help to reduce blood pressure, provide purpose and combat loneliness. And with crime on the rise in many areas, many dogs are finding homes because they may help deter criminals. Given these incentives for having a pet and an increasing number of older people and unmarried adults living alone, we can safely assume that pet ownership will continue to grow.

To ascertain the need for a pet-sitting service in your community, check the local Yellow Pages for listings of services or call veterinarians, groomers and pet stores to see if any such business exists. If you live in a rural area, consider that farmers and livestock owners often have a difficult time leaving home, so your service could be a real godsend. If there is already a service and you don't live in a sparsely populated area, there's probably room for more than one pet-sitting business.

Convinced that this business is for you? If so, the rest of this book is written to walk you through opening a professional and reputable pet-sitting service. I suggest that you read through it for a general overview of what the profession entails. Then go back and concentrate on specific chapters as you proceed with your own pet-sitting business.

2

Getting Started

RESOURCES

Today's new entrepreneur has a wealth of information and resources available that will assist and explain how to start a small business. It's important to spend time seeking out these resources so that you can learn as much as possible before opening your pet-sitting service. Careful preliminary planning and research will contribute greatly to the success of your business venture. "Doing your homework" is what I call this imperative first step.

Of course, reading this book is one of the wisest things you can do to understand what a pet-sitting business entails. Unlike other general business books, this publication specifically deals with running a particular kind of service. I only wish such a book had been available to me when I was pondering the idea and researching the field of pet sitting!

Still, it's wise to check out all available resources. Business books have become very popular, and you'll find many from which to choose at your local bookstore or library. They'll explain how to write a business plan, ways to raise business capital, and accounting for small businesses, among other things. Because of the wide availability of these books, I've intentionally omitted, or skimmed over, some of the subjects they cover. Research these topics thoroughly while considering opening your pet-sitting venture or exploring ways to improve your existing business.

While visiting your local library, check in the Periodicals Department for any magazine articles on pet sitting, small businesses or home-based businesses. Recently there has been tremendous public interest in these subjects, and you might find some good information in such articles.

The United States Small Business Administration (SBA) alone is a tremendous resource, and I strongly recommend that you contact your local SBA office for help in researching or starting your business. You'll be amazed at the wealth of information and assistance available from this governmental office. Since your tax dollars help fund this organization, why not take advantage of it? Write or call to get the address of a field office in your area.

United States Small Business Administration
1111 Eighteenth Street, N.W.
Sixth Floor
Washington, D.C. 20036
(202) 634–4950

Through the SBA, you can receive training and guidance on everything from the basics of starting a small business to developing records and bookkeeping systems to locating sources of financing to finding customers to determining a business site. The SBA also offers informative business development publications such as "Accounting Services for Small Service Firms," "Pricing Your Products and Services Profitably," "Planning and Goal Setting for Small Businesses," "Business Plan for Small Service Firms" and "Checklist for Going into Business." These are only a few of the many such publications available and you'll be wise to obtain and digest as much basic business knowledge as you can from these offerings. Some are available free of charge, while there is a nominal charge for others. All are certainly of value to the budding entrepreneur.

Excellent help can also be found from retired area executives who work through the SBA in a program called SCORE (Service Corp of Retired Executives). These retirees work on a volunteer basis to help those needing assistance and counseling in the world of business. The SCORE program has been operating since 1965 and is an asset to any community because of the invaluable expertise it provides. And the best part about it is that it's free! Check with your local SBA to determine if a SCORE group is located near you. You should also check with your local Chamber of Commerce, or any other business associations, to see if a similar volunteer program exists within their ranks.

Additional good local sources for information are the Chamber of Commerce, retail merchants' associations, Better Business Bureau and the Internal Revenue Service. If there's a community college nearby, check with them for upcoming classes that may be beneficial. Also check any local business magazine, journal or newspaper supplement that may list pertinent seminars, classes and lectures.

Since there is so much basic business information out there for the taking, learn all you can to operate your pet-sitting business efficiently and successfully. Acquiring a good working knowledge of the mechanics of business will certainly increase your chances of success.

MARKETING SURVEY

You're bound to see this step mentioned in other general business books, and it's a sound business idea worth emphasizing here. While to some extent the need for personalized, in-home pet care exists in all communities, you can ascertain the amount of interest in your area by conducting a marketing survey.

There are many ways to conduct such a survey. A good way to begin is to check the local Yellow Pages under "Kennels," "Pet Sitters" or "Sitting Services" to determine if any pet-sitting services already operate in your city or county. If not, you can be fairly confident that there is a need for this type of business.

You can better determine the level of interest or need by calling local veterinarians, groomers and pet store owners. Tell them about your plans, see if they know of anyone else offering such a service (some pet sitters don't advertise), and ask if they think this type of pet care would be well received by their clients. While you have their attention, ask if they would support your efforts by telling pet owners about your services once you're up and running.

If there is another pet sitter offering services, call and ask to speak with the person. Be honest and explain you're considering entering the field. The pet sitter may provide valuable insight about how busy the service is, whether business must be turned down, and the locations in which he or she works. Ask if the pet sitter might help you get started and offer a consultation fee. Remember that time and expertise are valuable commodities. A personal consultation with an experienced pet sitter may be worth its weight in gold.

You'll next want to approach pet owners and get their reaction to your proposed business. Find out how often they travel and what they presently do with their pets when they must leave home. Try to determine if they would be receptive to your service. Ask how much they'd be willing to pay for in-home care and what they'd expect from such a service.

You can conduct this portion of your survey by calling people cold from your telephone book and asking if they own a pet. Or you could obtain permission from a shopping center to approach a random group of shoppers with your questions. A better way, though, would be to acquire a list of clients (including addresses and telephone numbers) from your veterinarian or groomer. Since this sampling already owns pets, using it would be a more efficient way to conduct your research.

One pet sitter that I know purchased a mailing list from a pet magazine of subscribers in her city. She then sent out an initial customer query form to these prospective customers, informing them of her new business venture and inquiring about their interest in using her service. She included a preprinted post card that allowed them to answer her questions quickly and register their pet(s) with her company for future sittings. Not only did she receive lots of encouraging comments on these cards, but she got several definite customers before she even opened for business.

While doing your market research, don't forget to canvass your friends as well. You can usually count on friends to be honest because they want you to be happy and successful. They'll tell you if they think your idea is a good one, if the concept will go over in your area, and if you're cut out for this type of work. Invite their opinions and then listen objectively.

Once you've analyzed your market survey and determined that a pet-sitting business has merit, you'll feel more confident and energetic about opening a service. Be sure to save these results and statistics as they may be useful if you need to borrow operating capital to get your business started.

NAMING YOUR BUSINESS

Selecting a name for your pet-sitting service is an important first step. You'll need to put your thinking cap on, since this task is not as easy as one might think. Keep in mind that the name of your business creates a crucial first impression. Make sure that the name you choose conveys a positive image with which you'll be proud to be associated.

Name selection has become a more difficult task in recent years. When I opened my pet-sitting service in 1983, there were so

few services in operation that I had a wide choice of cute, catchy names. Today, with the increasing number of pet-sitting businesses, some names are trademarked and totally off limits for use by others. Therefore, it's a good idea to come up with several names for your business. In the event that your first choice is not available, you'll be ready with other options.

Once you've narrowed your names down to two or three favorites, you'll need to check with your local Register of Deeds to see if your first choice of name is in use by a business in your community. If the name is locally available to you, your next inquiry should be to the Secretary of State's office to determine if anyone in your state has registered a business under your preferred name. If not, you'll probably have free and clear right to do business under that name in your state.

At this point, the only hitch with being able to use the name would be if it was already trademarked with the United States Patent and Trademark Office in Washington, D.C. You can determine if there's a federal trademark on the name by visiting the United States Patent and Trademark Office and checking registrations, or by hiring a patent and trademark attorney to do this verification for you. In some cities there are also search services available that will check the name for a fee. Some libraries can do a computerized patent search for you. It's a specialized service and a fee may be involved.

While there is some expense involved in making sure you have the right to use a name, this can be a wise initial investment. I know of one pet sitter in Florida who had been doing business under a certain name for more than a year. She had established an excellent reputation and developed a devoted clientele. Out of the blue one day, a letter arrived from an attorney in the Midwest. He directed her to cease using her business's name immediately since it was federally trademarked (or owned) by his client. To make a long story short, the Florida pet sitter had to hire an attorney and found, indeed, she did not have the right to do business under her current name. The innocent mistake ended up being a very costly one; it was expensive to change all of her forms, stationery and business literature. Having to acclimate her clients to a new name was awkward as well. She told me that it would have been much cheaper to go through all the proper name-checking channels at the outset —not to mention the headaches she would have been spared.

Once you've decided on a name and found it available, you should consider how you can best protect the name for your business. Discuss how to do this with an attorney since it's a very serious subject. With the anticipated growth of the pet-sitting industry, you don't want any surprises in your mailbox in years to come. And, you'll want the legal backing to be able to protect your good name and reputation should another pet sitter try to infringe upon it.

One way to begin protection of your name is to go to your local Register of Deeds office and register the name as a business in your community. There will be a nominal charge for the registration.

BUSINESS LICENSE(S)

Your next step will be to check with your city and county offices to ascertain if a business license is required. Most communities issue these licenses for a small fee and a little paperwork, and some require that the license be visibly displayed in your place of business. As an upstanding citizen running a legitimate business, you'll need to obtain the proper business license(s) for your pet-sitting service. If you're unsure where to find out what is necessary regarding a license, check your local telephone directory under

14

"Government" or "City/County" headings for the appropriate offices.

OFFICE LOCATION

You'll also need to find a location for your pet-sitting service. The service, especially in the beginning, can easily be run from your home. If you have a spare bedroom, basement area or even a large closet available, this should be adequate. You need only a small space to set up your operation. In the past there have been tax advantages in operating a business from home. Since tax laws change frequently, you should get advice from a tax professional regarding any advantages in working at home.

If the idea of basing your business in your home is appealing, give careful thought to whether or not you can work well there. Can you discipline yourself to work, or will there be too many distractions or temptations to keep you from giving your business the time and effort required? Also, a large part of a pet-sitting service is conducted over the telephone, and calls may come at all hours. To keep work from disrupting your home life, you will have to be able to separate these two areas and think of the office as a workplace with its own hours.

Will you be running your pet-sitting service alone, or will you have a partner who will share the workload? If you have a partner, this may be a factor in determining where your office is located. A partner or office assistant may not feel comfortable or be able to work efficiently from your home. Will there be other pet-sitting staff members who will be traipsing in and out of your home? This could be bothersome to your family. And, are there small children who may decide to throw a tantrum while you're trying to sell your services to an inquirer? Give careful thought to your office location at the outset. Be sure of your location before having your business address and phone number printed; making changes on printed literature can be costly.

If you can work out the details to base your business in your home, it can be convenient and usually much cheaper to operate.

In fact, the establishment of home-based businesses of all types is a fast-growing phenomenon as more and more people discover the advantages of working at home.

But should you decide you'd prefer to locate your business outside your home, remember that you do not need the plushest surroundings for an office space. All you need at the beginning is an area large enough to accommodate a desk (or card table) for your phone, and a bookcase or shelf (or another card table) for your supplies, files and resource materials. It is rare for a customer to visit your office, so appearances are not critical. Look for the most reasonable rent in a convenient (for you) and safe area of town where you'll look forward to working. And, a final word of advice is to remember that rents and lease terms are not carved in stone. Don't be afraid to negotiate as you might find a landlord is willing to be flexible to secure a good tenant.

LEGAL STRUCTURE

Another important consideration in starting your pet-sitting service is how to legally structure your business. You may choose to set your business up as a sole proprietorship, a partnership or as a corporation. Tax consequences and liabilities vary with each of these legal structures. Seek advice from professionals (attorney, accountant, tax consultant) before deciding which structure is best for you and your business.

> *Note*: It is entirely possible to determine your business's legal structure and incorporate your business (if that is your choice) by yourself, just as you can do the research and legwork to register your business's name and obtain business licenses. This way you save attorney fees and lower your start-up costs. However, I strongly recommend that you at least consult with an attorney regarding these business matters and decisions. Usually there's little or no charge for a consultation, and the discussion will help you to make more informed decisions about your business. A reliable attorney and accountant can be instrumental in your business's well-being. You are wise to cultivate good relationships with both at the very outset of your new venture.

In other words, let key people do what they do best to help you do your best.

FINDING AN ACCOUNTANT

Here again, unless you're an experienced bookkeeper, it is advisable to find an accountant to assist you with the necessary recordkeeping for your pet-sitting service. Look for one who specializes in accounting for small businesses, as that's what you'll be the first few years anyway. An accountant will help you to set up your books, do your payroll and apply for any necessary identification numbers. An accountant can also save you some running around by supplying you with forms you'll need, such as state and federal payroll tax forms. Although accounting procedures may at first seem overwhelming to a new business owner, a good accountant will soon have you trained and knowledgeable about the financial side of your business.

It's wise to shop around when searching for an accountant. Ask other business owners for recommendations and then interview a few accountants before making a decision. Accounting fees and expertise vary, so don't be shy in requesting fees, credentials and references from candidates. Make sure that the individual is someone you feel you can trust and get along with. If you should find yourself unhappy with the accountant you choose to work with initially, remember that you are not locked into his or her services, and you can take your business elsewhere.

SELECTING A BANK

A business checking account is necessary for your pet-sitting service. Here again, it pays to shop around before making a decision. Different banks offer various features and hours of operation. You should also take into account how conveniently located the bank is. Once your pet-sitting services become popular, you'll have little time to waste when making bank deposits. Some banks advertise specifically to attract small business owners. Find out what, if any, services they provide that may directly benefit you.

Explore the possibility of obtaining a credit card exclusively for your business's use. In today's business world, a credit card can come in handy when making large purchases for your business, traveling to seminars or simply entertaining clients. Also, by paying your account on time, the credit card helps you to establish a credit history for your business.

So, spend some time exploring your banking options down to the last details of what type of checks and deposit slips are available. It's important to allot time to this during your preplanning stages because after your business is up and running, your time truly does become more limited.

INSURANCE

It is smart and advisable to obtain liability insurance and a dishonesty bond to cover you and any other pet sitters working in your business. Hopefully, you'll never need to use this insurance, but having the coverage will give you and your customers peace of

mind. Being bonded and insured speaks well for the professionalism and integrity of your business. And, very importantly, it is often a selling point to interested but hesitant customers.

Since the first edition of this book appeared, many people have written to me, indicating that they have had a difficult time finding commercial liability insurance for their pet-sitting businesses. I can empathize with them because I, too, had a difficult time obtaining such insurance when I first opened my service.

The reason it has been difficult to find coverage is because pet sitting is a relatively new profession with unique insurance needs. A pet-sitting business is unlike a kennel operation that insures its premises for accidents and damages. Instead, a pet sitter needs protection that insures the premises of each client where he or she is conducting business. Our need is similar to that of a janitorial or cleaning service that visits various locations for the performance of duties. However, our liability coverage also needs to extend to the animals entrusted to our care.

Many insurance companies have never heard of the pet-sitting industry and, therefore, won't have a policy already available to meet your specific needs. But that doesn't mean an insurance policy tailored to your business cannot be created. Just be prepared to explain the nature of the pet-sitting business and ask if a policy can be designed specifically for you. If you have an insurance agent with whom you've done business in the past, contact him or her first. If the agent has written your automobile or homeowner's in-surance, he or she already knows a little about you. In order to keep your business, the agent may be more willing to seek out the proper coverage for your pet-sitting business.

Since I beat the bushes for insurance in 1983, I've seen some increase in the number of insurance companies that are willing to provide coverage to our new industry. Still, more improvement is needed, and this should come about as the number of reputable pet sitters grows throughout the country. As our industry becomes more widely known and establishes more credibility, insurers will begin to see pet sitters as a good business risk. Hopefully, a wider range of coverages will result in more competitive policy rates. For the near future, though, you can most likely expect insurance coverage to be your most expensive cost of doing business. Unfortunately, we live in a time marked by a steady escalation in the number of lawsuits. This lawsuit madness has made liability insurance a necessary evil for business owners, and at the same time it has made the cost of protection exorbitant.

While surveying your insurance prospects, you should also investigate purchasing an automobile rider that would provide additional insurance coverage in the event of an automobile accident when pet sitting. This type of coverage kicks in only if the pet sitter's personal automobile insurance coverage is not adequate for damages incurred.

As your business grows, you may want to review your life insurance coverage. Make sure that it would be adequate to keep your business going in the event of your death, and that it would cover any debts owed by your business for which your estate may be accountable. Life insurance may not have been important to you before, but it is something you should consider as a business owner.

If you'll be hiring employees to help you with pet sitting visits, you'll also need to investigate Worker's Compensation insurance. Most states require some form of this insurance, and your insurance agent or state Department of Labor can tell you what applies to your business. This type of insurance covers the employees of a business should they be injured while working.

You should shop around for insurance coverage; you may be surprised to find how much coverages and rates can vary. Besides, your phone calls will help to educate more insurance agents about our growing industry. And who knows? The agent may be a local pet owner who'd be interested in using your service!

BASIC OFFICE SUPPLIES AND FURNISHINGS

There are a few basic furnishings and supplies you'll need for your business office before officially opening your pet-sitting service. Try to keep your office materials to a minimum, as that reduces overhead costs. These savings can be passed along to your customers in lower pet-sitting rates. Lower rates may result in a higher volume of customers, which will contribute to the success of your business.

Recommended Office Basics Include:

- A TABLE OR DESK
- CHAIR(S)
- BOOKCASE (shelf or space for supplies)
- TELEPHONE (NOTE: please see discussion on telephone at the end of this chapter.)
- TELEPHONE ANSWERING MACHINE OR ANSWERING SERVICE
- CITY MAPS—one for the office and one for your car. A city map is helpful for determining service routes, as well as for getting you to your clients' homes.
- CALCULATOR—a basic model that adds, subtracts, multiplies and divides should suffice.
- NAME-AND-ADDRESS RUBBER STAMP—handy for endorsing checks and preaddressing envelopes for the customers to use when paying. Don't forget the necessary ink pad.
- TYPEWRITER OR COMPUTER WITH WORD-PROCESSING PROGRAM—either one of these is nice but is not absolutely necessary. If you don't have access to one, or don't type, you can hire a typist (look in the newspaper classified ads or Yellow Pages). And you could have any necessary forms typeset at a printing company. This is more expensive but looks much nicer and more professional.
- FILING CABINET—a must for storing paperwork (forms, literature, advertising . . .) associated with your business.
- SCHEDULE BOOK AND CALENDAR—these are absolutely necessary to keep up with customer appointments, sitting assignments, etc. WRITE IT DOWN or you'll find yourself needing to pick up two sets of housekeys at the same time on opposite ends of town . . . which is a little hard to do.
- REFERENCE BOOKS ON VARIOUS PETS—some of these may be available from your local library but it's best to form your own collection. Familiarize yourself with different types of animals and various breeds. When a customer calls and asks what you charge for caring for a Maltese, you'll know it's a dog and not a falcon!
- ANY FIRST-AID SUPPLIES FOR PET EMERGENCIES THAT YOU MAY WISH TO HAVE ON HAND.

Paper Supplies You'll Need Are:

- INDEX CARDS AND STORAGE BOX.

- STATIONERY—professionally printed with your business name, address, phone number and any logo or slogan you wish to associate with your business.

- ENVELOPES MATCHING YOUR STATIONERY—you may want to pick a color(s) and then use it (or them) everywhere your name is seen. The repetition will help make your business recognizable to your public.

- ENVELOPES—white business envelopes you can preaddress (with your rubber stamp) for your customers to remit payment.

- BUSINESS CARDS—professionally printed as these will be used a lot to advertise your business. And you do want them to look nice and convey a good first impression to potential clients. They are relatively inexpensive.

- A FLYER OR BROCHURE—giving basic information about what your service provides. This is a valuable advertising tool that you'll use often. This item is discussed in more detail in Chapter 5, ''Advertising.''

- NOTEPADS—these can be plain or matching your other stationery. They will be used primarily for leaving your clients notes and, of course, for phone messages.

- ACCOUNTING LEDGER—this is a columnar book that your accountant most likely will supply and explain to you.

- FIVE-COLUMNAR ACCOUNTING PAD—this ledger is available in most office supply stores. These sheets contain lined pages that you can use to chart sitter schedules. (You may choose to purchase sitter schedule sheets that I've developed for New Beginnings—please see the Addenda for details on how to order.)

- BUSINESS FORMS—you'll at least need a well-thought-out service contract for your business, and there are other forms that will be helpful as well. These are discussed in Chapter 7, ''Useful Business Forms.''

Other standard office supplies you'll need include:

- pens and pencils
- scissors
- postage stamps
- paper clips
- file folders
- hanging file folders
- ruler
- tape
- folder and housekey labels
- stapler
- staple remover
- correction fluid

Your office supplies need not be brand new. If you have an extra pair of scissors around the house, loan them to your business. For anything you do purchase, be sure and keep the receipt. Any legitimate office and business expenses will need to be accounted for at tax time.

Keep your business supplies as pet-related as possible. Your logo, stationery and business cards, for example, can easily be designed to reflect the nature of your business. Try to order checks from your bank that have pets pictured on them. Also, purchase stamps that feature pets or wildlife. I have used such checks and stamps for years and have found that people really do notice the coordinated details of my business. Just be sure not to sacrifice professionalism for what I call "cutesiness."

In conclusion, a word about your business telephone. Some pet sitters operating from home have made the mistake of using their personal telephone number as their business line. For several reasons, this is not such a good idea. First, your telephone company will not appreciate your disregard for their policy on business lines, and there could even be a tariff violation or penalty if it learns of your home-based business. Secondly, while a business line does normally cost more than a residence line, you also usually get a free Yellow Page listing for your business. This exposure can really help to increase the calls you'll receive for service. After all, if you've named your business "XYZ Pet Sitters" but your phone number is only listed under your name, Mary Doe, how is the public going to find you? Your credibility as a reputable business could be damaged by a potential client's inability to find your number in the phone book or through information. Thirdly, as your business grows, your phone will be ringing more and more. Calls will come in at all hours. Since you'll have no way of knowing whether the call is of a personal or business nature, you'll find yourself answering the phone and possibly beginning to feel that you have no privacy. Prevent this problem by ordering a legitimate business line from the outset of your pet-sitting venture. That way, you can distinguish callers and answer your business line only during your regularly scheduled office hours. And finally, your business's phone bill will be an expense of doing business and, as such, can be claimed on your income tax return. By having a separate billing for your business line, your record and receipt keeping will also be a much easier task.

> *Note*: Many customers will memorize your business's phone number. Get a number that you plan to keep for years to come and one that's easy to remember as well. Have the entire phone number or the last four digits spell out "PETS" or "DOGS" or "CATS" or "LOVE"—something identifiable with your service!

You may be wondering if you'll need either a telephone answering machine or personal answering service for your business. Yes, you will need one of these methods for taking messages. The merits of each will be discussed in the chapter that follows.

3

Office Procedures

CUSTOMER CARD SYSTEM

Whether you work alone or you have twelve sitters working with you, you'll need an organized system in order to run your office efficiently. The system developed and used successfully in my office may seem simple and elementary, but it works. You may wish to expand or improve upon it, but it will provide a means of getting started.

First, the index cards and storage box (mentioned in my section "Basic Office Supplies") make up your customer card box. When receiving calls for pet-sitting services, you'll need to make a customer card for each client. The sample shown here indicates some of the pertinent information you should gather when the reservation is made. Write this data in pencil to allow for any necessary changes. You'll find that last names, addresses, phone numbers and even pets do change.

After you've checked the schedules and assigned a sitter to the job, notify the customer regarding who his or her sitter will be and pencil in the sitter's name in the right-hand corner of the card.

```
┌─────────────────────────────────────────────────────────────┐
│                                                               │
│    Customer Name                        Sitter's Name         │
│    Address                                                    │
│    City, State  Zip Code                                      │
│                                                               │
│    Home Phone Number:                                         │
│    Work Phone Number:                                         │
│                                                               │
│    Type of Pets:                        Price:                │
│    Visits Requested Per Day:                                  │
│    How Did You Hear About Our Service?                        │
│    Dates  of  Services:                                       │
│                                                               │
└─────────────────────────────────────────────────────────────┘
```

Place the card in a stack of "jobs to notify sitters about" by the telephone.

SITTER SCHEDULE SHEETS

After promptly contacting the appropriate sitter for each job, turn to your sitter schedule sheets. A schedule is made on each sitter using the five-columnar accounting pad mentioned in my section "Basic Office Supplies." The sample below shows how I suggest you label your assignment sheets. *Only after* you've given the sitter information about the upcoming assignment do you fill in the customer's name and dates of the assignment on the sheet. This is your

<u>Sitter Schedule Sheet</u>

Sitter's Name,
Address, and Phone Number
Areas of Service Route

Customer Name	Dates of Service	Job Completed	Payment Received	Sitter Paid	New★ Customer?
K. Smith	7/1/86 7/7/86	✔	7/10/86 54.00	✔ 8/1/86	★

Vacation of Sitter 8/8/86 8/15/86
12/10/86 12/12/86

way of making sure you've assigned it. Then place the customer card in a designated space for pending jobs, sorted by the month and week in which they occur.

Having an assignment sheet for each sitter permits you to see at a glance how many jobs he or she has and guards against over-booking a person. You'll also need to fill in any vacation time or other dates of unavailability on each sheet to help you in assigning jobs.

The next step is to check customer cards daily in the ongoing/pending stacks to see which jobs have ended. I then place these cards vertically and alphabetically in my customer card box. This tells me the jobs are finished but are not yet paid for. As payments arrive in the office, I record the date and amount of payment. Then the card is turned horizontally in the customer card box. I then turn to the sitter's assignment sheet and write in the date and amount paid by the customer. After endorsing the checks, I make my bank deposit.

When it's time to write payroll or commission checks, you'll use the "payment received" column on the sitter schedule sheets. I always write the date the customer's check was received in this column. By referring to this column each month, I can easily see for which jobs the sitter is due payment. I also write in the date the sitter is compensated in the "sitter paid" column. And this, in a nutshell, is the system I've used in my pet-sitting service. Simple enough? To clarify the steps even further, a flow chart illustrating my system is shown.

UNPAID ACCOUNTS   **PAID ACCOUNTS**

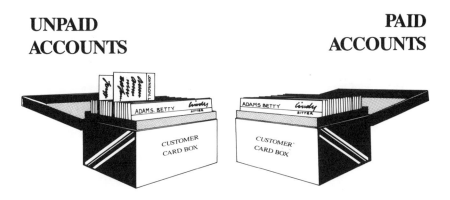

Office Procedures Flow Chart

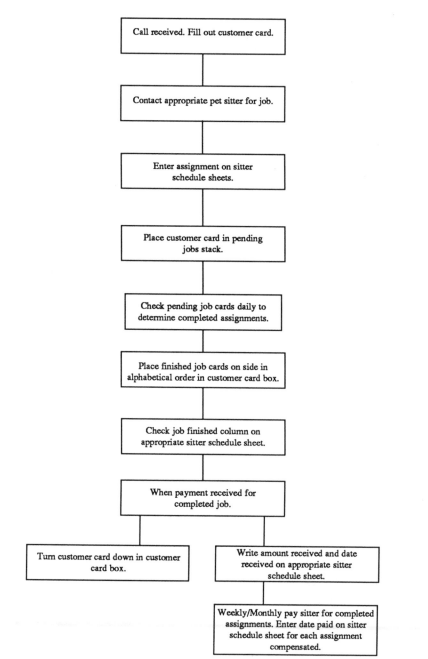

Call received. Fill out customer card.

Contact appropriate pet sitter for job.

Enter assignment on sitter schedule sheets.

Place customer card in pending jobs stack.

Check pending job cards daily to determine completed assignments.

Place finished job cards on side in alphabetical order in customer card box.

Check job finished column on appropriate sitter schedule sheet.

When payment received for completed job.

Turn customer card down in customer card box.

Write amount received and date received on appropriate sitter schedule sheet.

Weekly/Monthly pay sitter for completed assignments. Enter date paid on sitter schedule sheet for each assignment compensated.

Note: If you're treating your pet sitters as independent contractors, your business and accounting procedures will need to be structured differently to meet the guidelines set forth by the Internal Revenue Service. A knowledgeable accountant can explain the advantages and disadvantages of using independent contractors for assignments and how to do your recordkeeping if this is the staffing method you choose.

HANDLING DELINQUENT ACCOUNTS

By keeping the customer cards turned vertically on their side until payment is received, it's easy to do a weekly check to see if any accounts are becoming delinquent. If more than an acceptable amount of time for payment has passed, you may want to call the customer or mail out a friendly past due letter. Samples of such a letter follow.

Delinquent Account Letter #1

Dear Client:

A review of our records indicates a delinquent balance on your account of $ _____. This amount is due for our pet-sitting services provided by Molly Smith, from July 7 through 14, 1991. We hope this has simply been an oversight on your part. We enjoyed caring for your pet(s) and would like to continue sitting for you in the future. Therefore, we thank you in advance for remitting payment to us within the next five days.

Very truly yours,

XYZ Pet Sitters, Inc.

Delinquent Account Letter #2

Dear (client's name):

A review of our records shows that you owe a balance of_____ for XYZ Pet Sitters, Inc., services rendered_____through_____. We believe there are two sides to every story, so if you'll be so kind as to listen to our side, we'll listen to your side.

OUR SIDE	YOUR SIDE
We provided XYZ Pet Sitter services which you requested in a reliable, trustworthy and caring manner. Our service contract plainly states that payment is due within 3 days after a customer returns from a trip. We regret that in an effort to reduce our overhead costs and keep our service affordable, we are not able to extend credit.	
If you were pleased with our services, we shall appreciate your prompt remittance of fees owed. If you were not pleased, we shall appreciate hearing your side in the right-hand column of this page.	
We appreciate your cooperation and hope that you've "just forgotten" about your balance owed.	
We look forward to your continued business.	

Very truly yours,

XYZ Pet Sitters, Inc.

My experience has shown, though, that delinquent accounts are not much of a problem; 99.9% of my customers promptly pay their bills after using our services. I like to think that our excellent collection record is a direct reflection on the quality of our service. Perhaps clients are so pleased that they immediately pay their bills in order to stay on our good side. I've also come to believe through the years that people who love their pets enough to hire a pet sitter are not the kind of people who write bad checks or ignore their financial obligations.

The occasional straggler I've had has usually been a client

who travels so frequently that, I'm sure, he or she had simply not been home long enough to sit down and pay all the bills. The stragglers, though, almost always come through and usually include a nice tip as an apology for their lateness. Sometimes it pays to be flexible with your payment terms for unusual situations.

To protect myself against these late or nonpaying customers, I have included a clause in our service contract that says when payment is due and notes that a monthly interest rate will be charged on unpaid accounts in excess of thirty days. I also state that a penalty will be charged on any checks returned from the bank. Perhaps I've been lucky, but since establishing my business I've had very few checks returned from the bank for insufficient funds. After I notified the clients, they immediately made the checks good.

There are some pet sitters who require full payment in advance, especially from new clients. While this idea has merit and may be more of a necessity in large metropolitan areas, I've never instituted the practice in my business. It's my belief that pet owners should be able to use the service, make sure they are pleased, and then pay their bill in a timely manner. I always try to put myself in the client's shoes, and there's something disconcerting to me about being required to pay in advance for something that I may not be happy with. New clients in particular may feel uneasy about up-front payment. However, once they try your service and are pleased, don't be surprised to find that they leave advance payment for you on the kitchen counter for subsequent home visits.

The only situation in which I do require any advance payment is for lengthy assignments that exceed a certain dollar amount. When this is the case, I insist that one-half of the bill be paid. My reasoning here is that the longer the assignment, the greater the chance for extra expense: more food or supplies may be needed; the pet may become ill and require veterinary care; or something could go wrong at the home, requiring the services of a plumber or electrician. Should any of these things occur, we have money from the client with which to cover these costs without dipping into our company's bank account. Any additional money owed by the client can then be paid upon his or her return. It's not unreasonable to require a deposit on lengthy assignments; however, it is your business, so you'll need to set your own payment policy and be sure that it is one with which you can live.

Should you have any problem or dispute in collecting payment from a client, remember that you do have the recourse of small claims court. (Small claims court is where a magistrate hears cases in which the amount involved is usually less than $1,500.00.) Sometimes just threatening to take the client to court is enough to secure payment. But, if necessary, don't hesitate to use the recourse of small claims court. Taking someone who owes you money to court is a simple, straightforward process, and relatively inexpensive. The only inconvenience may be the time required to sit in court until your case can be presented. So, if you believe in the job that you did for the client and have exhausted other civil means of collecting the payment rightfully due you, by all means, take the client to court.

Remember that a signed service contract authorizing your services is critical when proving nonpayment for services requested and rendered. Make sure you get the client's signature for each assignment, or have a signed authorization from the client permitting you to take their telephone reservations and instructions. Otherwise, you may have a very weak case should small claims court become necessary.

TELEPHONE TECHNIQUES

The telephone plays a vital role in your business since the majority of your business is handled over the telephone. Customers call to get information about your service and to book your services. A phone conversation may be the first impression a client gets of your business so telephone etiquette is extremely important. Your local telephone company may provide you with business phone tips, so ask if it also provides business etiquette advice. Here are some pointers I can share with you:

- Answer your phone quickly—after two rings if possible.
- Identify your company name and who's speaking (XYZ Pet Sitting Service, Jane Smith speaking).

- Speak in a courteous, friendly, confident tone.
- Smile as you speak! You may feel silly at first, but it really reflects in your tone of voice.
- Provide as much information as possible about your service.
- Patiently try to answer all of the client's questions. It's only natural for a potential new client to have some reservations about using your service and allowing a stranger into the home.
- When using an answering machine, personalize your message and say *when* calls will be returned.
- Return customer calls promptly. This goes for you and your sitters.
- Use the phone to obtain as much initial information as possible about an assignment. Fill out your customer card completely during the phone conversation.
- When a sitting assignment is finished, use the phone to determine if a client is satisfied with your company's service.

I can't stress enough how important telephone skills are in this type of business. So practice and sharpen yours to ensure the success of your pet-sitting venture.

Sample Narrative

(For giving out information over the telephone about your services)

Question: Can you tell me a little about your service?

Answer: What we do is to provide personalized home pet care. We actually come to your home so that you are able to leave your pet in familiar surroundings. We try to follow your routine as closely as possible with your pet. This involves feeding and watering, exercising and giving any medication your pet may require. We also spend what we call quality time with your pet - just playing, petting or loving it so that it receives personal attention while you're away. We're happy to keep an eye on your home and at the same time do things such as bringing in mail and newspapers, alternating lights, opening and closing curtains and blinds, watering plants - trying to give your home a lived-in look. Our sitters are bonded and insured, and our charges are based upon the type of pets you have and the number of visits made. Four days notice is required for our services.

ANSWERING MACHINES VERSUS PERSONAL ANSWERING SERVICES

Since pet sitting involves making visits to your clients' homes, it will be impossible for you to answer your business telephone at all times. Since you don't want to miss a call, you'll need some reliable way for callers to leave you messages. Your most likely options are to purchase a dependable answering machine or employ a personal answering service. There are advantages and disadvantages to both methods.

First, a personal answering service gives your business just what the name implies, a personal touch. When you can't be by the phone, your calls are forwarded to the answering service you've hired. A person answers your calls and takes messages. Upon returning to your office, you simply call the service and receive your messages. One problem with this method is that the caller who wants to talk to someone right away may be frustrated by reaching a person who can't do anything more than take a message. The phone operators just aren't qualified, authorized or paid to offer specific information about your services. The other negative element is the cost. It is very nice to have calls answered and messages taken, but there's a price involved for this personal service. If there are several answering services in your community, you should shop around, as their prices and services do vary. It's a good idea to check with some of their clients, making sure they are satisfied with the service.

The answering machine has really grown in popularity during recent years. It used to be that most everyone hated these machines and refused to leave messages on them. That's changed drastically as people have found that in this busy day and age they just can't function well without them. And our society is becoming accustomed to talking to a machine. Also, the price of answering machines has come down, making them an affordable convenience in many homes today. Thus, the answering machine is a viable and very economical means of message-taking for the small business. It also allows you to customize or personalize your outgoing messages to fit your business needs or seasonal changes. Some examples of this are shown on page 36.

The biggest disadvantage of an answering machine is probably the fact that it can malfunction. Lightning may run in on one during a storm or, unbeknownst to you, your tapes may simply wear out, causing you to lose valuable messages. Fortunately, these instances are few and far between. But they are risks to consider when making this important decision for your business.

Whichever method you choose for your business, be sure that calls are professionally answered and promptly returned.

Note: The nice thing about a telephone answering machine is the fact that your outgoing message can be changed easily to accommodate your scheduled office hours, seasons or holidays. If you want to be creative, you can even have a "leave your message after you hear the BARK, MEOW, etc."

Sample Answering Machine Messages

Sample Everyday Message:

This is XYZ Pet Sitters' answering machine. Our office hours are from _____ to _____ daily /Monday-Friday (whatever yours are). If you need information about our service, please leave your name and daytime phone number. If you are a client returning home from a trip, please leave your name and a brief message. Thank you for calling XYZ Pet Sitters.

Sample Holiday Messages:

Merry Christmas! This is XYZ Pet Sitters' answering machine. Our office hours are _____ to _____ Monday-Friday. If you would like information about our service, please leave your name and phone number where you can be reached during these hours. We are rapidly becoming booked for the Christmas holidays, so please make your reservations early to assure service. Thank you for calling.

Merry Christmas! We're out walking Santa's reindeer now and can't personally take your call—so we hope you'll talk to our machine. We're completely booked for the Christmas holidays through December 27. Our office is closed until 2 p.m. December 28. We still have a few openings for New Year's and are also taking January reservations at this time. Please leave your name and number after you hear the beep, and we'll return your call between 2 and 5 p.m. on the next business day. Thanks for calling and Happy Holidays.

Sample Message for Inclement Weather:

This is XYZ Pet Sitters. Our office is closed due to the inclement weather. For those with reservations, sitters will be making rounds as road conditions permit safe travel. Messages will be monitored, so if you have a cancellation, require information or need to make a reservation, please leave your name and number and we'll return your call as soon as possible. Begin your message after you hear the beep. Thanks for calling.

DETERMINING SERVICE ROUTES

An important part of your preplanning involves deciding where you'll provide pet-sitting services in your community. Initially, you may wish to start by working alone and sitting within a five-mile radius of your home. This would allow you the opportunity to make sure you enjoy this type of business without incurring the added responsibility of recruiting, training and managing other sitters.

However, if you are ready for the challenge of a larger staff and service area and feel the demand for pet sitters exists in your community—then go for it! In three years' time, I went from two sitters (one being me) to thirty. Obtain a current map of your city or town (often available from the Chamber of Commerce, Town Hall or real estate offices) and then familiarize yourself with it. It is helpful if you are an established member of the community. Then you are probably familiar with economic boundaries, growth trends, the safer areas and, of course, shortcuts around town. If you are new to the community, this is a great way to learn your way around, plus meet many neighbors and area residents.

There are many ways to decide where you'll provide pet-sitting services. You can split your territories into north, south, east, west routes; by zip codes or neighborhoods; by subdivisions or condominium complexes, etc. Keep in mind the travel involved; if your routes are too extended, your profit may be eaten up in gasoline costs. Define which areas you'll cover and then make sure you're staffed to offer services within them. Also, make sure that your advertising defines the areas in which you sit. Otherwise, you'll waste a lot of time answering calls and explaining that your service doesn't extend to the caller's neighborhood.

SETTING PRICES

This can be a difficult task for the new pet sitter because, unfortunately, there's no magic formula for establishing a price structure for your service. There are some guidelines, though, that will assist you as you tackle this important task.

First of all, do some basic research in your community. Spend a few hours calling area boarding kennels, veterinarians and any other pet-sitting services to see what they charge for keeping various animals. This will tell you what the going rates are for pet care and also tell you who your competition is. The cost of living in different parts of the country will greatly affect the charges for such services. Make notes on your findings for comparison and future reference.

Secondly, decide upon the territories involved for each sitter's service route and the traveling distance rounds will entail. If personal vehicles will be used by sitters, your prices will need to account for gasoline and wear and tear on their vehicles. The simplest way to calculate this is to use the federal government's approved reimbursement per mile which, as of this writing, is $0.275 per mile. If a sitter is responsible for a five-mile radius sitting zone, then the sitter may average around ten miles of travel, or $2.75 in gasoline and wear-and-tear costs. This amount needs to be added to your prices on a per-job basis. A sitter may be caring for only one home and pet and still drive five miles to and from the job. Another time, the sitter may be stopping to care for five customers' homes and pets along the same five-mile route. But, whether it's one stop or five, the same amount of gasoline and wear on the car is involved and should be factored into your fee. By using the government's price per mile, you have something concrete and substantiated on which to base this fee. If public transportation is used to make service rounds, the cost and time involved will need to be considered when setting your prices. (Another option is to charge separately for gas or transportation costs. I personally find this method complicated and confusing for the client, as well as for the pet sitter!)

Thirdly, time is another important factor to be weighed in establishing your fees. I estimate that my sitters spend five to seven minutes in getting to a home, a minimum of thirty minutes in the home, and five to seven minutes returning from the assignment or traveling to the next customer's home. This averages out to about forty-five minutes per home. The time and price increase per home if there's more than one pet involved. I also consider the minimum hourly wage and try to make sure that the sitter gets a reasonable wage for the time, responsibility, risk and occasional inconvenience involved in pet sitting. You'll want your wage to be high enough so that the pet-sitter position appeals to the caliber of person you want working for you.

You'll also want to do some arithmetic to anticipate what the overhead costs of your business will be. After you've gotten estimates on rent, utilities, telephone, printed literature, insurance, bonding, advertising, etc., figure what you'll need to make on a monthly basis to at least cover these costs, much less pay a salary to yourself and any office help you'll need. To allow you to meet these expenses, a flat overhead cost, as well as a margin of profit, will need to be factored into each established fee.

The final figure(s) for the fee may seem high at first, but remember this is a personalized service you'll be providing. Don't undersell yourself or the valuable services offered by a pet sitter. After all, you're making it much easier for a pet owner to leave home with peace of mind. On the other hand, be realistic in setting your prices—don't price yourself out of reach. While you can go up or down on your prices, setting your fees and sticking to them will create credibility and give you a more professional image. So it's crucial for you to do your homework. Some trial and error may be involved, and your public will quickly let you know if you're too high or too low. Put forth the effort required to be on the mark and competitively priced.

Note: Whenever possible, it is always best to adhere to your price structure. However, there will be times when you may increase a fee or offer a discount. Occasionally, someone may book services who lives two doors away or across the street from you or the pet sitter. With no gasoline or great distance involved in the job, you may feel a smaller fee is appropriate, or your sitter may request a lowered rate for the customer. On the other hand, a customer may have more than what's deemed normal in houseplants (like a greenhouse) that will need watering. If what's needed in a home requires more than the average amount of time you have calculated in your fees, then, of course, you'll raise your fees accordingly. However, something such as a litter of kittens that are still feeding from their mother may not require any additional efforts of a pet sitter, so you should not treat them as additional cats in your sitting fees. Most of your calls will involve routine pets and the typical care that is included in your established fees. Whenever there is a question, I always try to give the customer a minimum and maximum ballpark figure for services. I then allow the sitter to make the final determination about fees after seeing what the job entails.

When setting your prices and payment policy, you'll need to determine at the outset what you'll accept for payment. Will you accept cash only, cash and personal checks, or will your customers have the option of paying by credit card? As of this writing, I know of very few pet sitters who accept credit cards in their businesses. Although we live in a so-called world of plastic, the general consensus seems to be that the 3–5 percent service charge for merchants makes this option cost prohibitive to small business owners, which most pet sitters are. If your customers repeatedly request this payment option, it may be something you'll want to look into as your business grows.

COMPENSATING SITTERS

When setting the pay rate or commission splits for sitters working in your organization, keep in mind the overhead costs, along with the profit you want the business to realize. You'll need to be fair, though, in compensating your staff members. Their time, travel and work are extremely important to your reputation and success. Although the work is usually very enjoyable, few pet lovers can afford to do it for nominal pay. Set your pay scale so that it is competitive and motivates sitters to take pride and do a good job as representatives of your company.

Some pet-sitting services pay by the assignment and others pay on an hourly basis; there is no right or wrong way. Just make sure that what you pay is enough to attract the kind of dependable and trustworthy sitters your business needs.

HANDLING CUSTOMER COMPLAINTS

If you have done a good job in recruiting pet sitters, and you track their performance with rating forms or telephone follow-ups, you should have few, if any, complaints. However, regardless of how terrific your service is, sooner or later you're bound to run into that customer who lives to complain. Or perhaps there will be a legitimate problem, and the customer will be justified in criticizing your service or sitter. To help you deal with such confrontation, I am noting the way I've managed the handful of complaints against my business through the years.

- I always listen open-mindedly to what the customer has to say. Believing in the people who sit for my organization, I convey to the customer my surprise and concern about the complaint.
- I next express my sincere regret about the complaint and ask for the opportunity to discuss the problem with the sitter involved, believing that there are two sides to every story.
- I assure the client I'll be back in touch with him or her promptly and also thank the client for bringing this concern to my attention.
- Then, I do reach the sitter involved as quickly as possible and attempt to get to the bottom of the complaint.

If after hearing both sides of a story, I feel that the sitter was in error, I apologize profusely to the client and waive or reduce payment for services rendered. If I feel the complaint is not justified, I explain to the client the sitter's and business's stand or defense in the matter, and I hope that he or she understands our viewpoint or action. I've come to realize there are some people that you can never please and that I'm better off without their business. Fortunately, these people are few and far between and, as the owner of your business, you do have the right to refuse your services to them.

Again, knowing your sitters helps in these instances. You probably won't know most of your customers, but if you know and feel good about your sitters, you can believe, trust and defend their actions. It's extremely important to recruit and hire only those individuals who will be assets to your business. Excellent sitters are the key to very few complaints and the success of your service.

> *Note*: It's important to have your sitters make you aware of any problems they encounter on a sitting assignment. This way you'll be better informed and able to deal more knowledgeably with a complaint. Better yet is for you or your sitter to call the customer and discuss a situation before it leads to a complaint. The daily notes to a client left by sitters are also used in explaining problems and how they were handled, which can prevent a complaint. And, always, I believe honesty is the best policy.

USING A COMPUTER

The office procedures described earlier in this chapter have worked well and enabled me to operate my business efficiently for several years. However, as my business and customer base grew, my husband convinced me that a computer would be a labor-saving and timesaving addition to my office. So, a few years ago, I reluctantly purchased a computer and a letter-quality printer.

My husband was right (as usual), and I quickly found that a computer can be used in myriad ways. It can be used to maintain a mailing list for any business correspondence, advertising or newsletters. It can be used to build a customer database. If you enter the ways clients learned of your service in a file, you can get a count of these every three or six months to see what advertising is working for you. Or, you can enter all customer complaints in a file and print these out every so often to make sure you're not overlooking a recurring problem. A computer can take care of many bookkeeping chores, keeping track of paid and unpaid accounts and business expenses. Another benefit is that it can be used to maintain and print out sitter assignment sheets and customer cards.

Still, a computer is not an essential piece of equipment for a pet-sitting business, especially in the beginning. If you already have one, by all means, use it in your business. But I wouldn't recommend this purchase as vital until you're established and operating profitably. When you reach a customer base of several hundred people, you may find the computer to be more of a necessity.

Note: My husband has written a software application program specifically designed for pet-sitting companies. The PET-SIT application is to be used with the versatile PFS:FILE software program. For ordering information, please see the Addenda of this book.

4

Personnel

FINDING AND QUALIFYING PET SITTERS

The most critical factor to your success is the selection of the pet sitters who join your organization. You know your own abilities and that you will do a wonderful job of pet sitting, but you have to be absolutely sure you find the right people to help you. There is much at stake in this business of caring for other people's pets and homes, so recruiting personnel is an area that deserves careful thought and consideration.

What do you look for in potential pet sitters? My experience has shown they need to be:

- true pet lovers
- dependable and reliable
- trustworthy individuals
- able to provide their own transportation and telephone
- comfortable and happy meeting the public

With these criteria in mind, you might try approaching your friends, family and neighbors to ask if they can think of anyone to recruit. Chances are that one of them will volunteer to help, and you will have your first employee! Be sure to explain, however, that this will be a business relationship with no special privileges.

If possible, try to find sitters who come highly recommended from someone whose opinion you trust. If you do not know applicants, it's smart to learn as much about them as you can. Other excellent sources of pet sitters are local kennel clubs, cat clubs and humane societies. Possibly some of their members will be interested in pet sitting or will know of others who would be good candidates. Either call or write to these groups, explaining your service and need for additional pet sitters. The letter I've used for this purpose is shown below.

Humane Society, Kennel Club Letter

Dear Humane Society members:

Enclosed you will find information explaining our new business, XYZ Pet Sitters, Inc. Our service is available to pet owners in the city and the surrounding areas. We would appreciate it if you would announce our service at your next meeting.

We also wish to support your organization. Please send us information regarding membership at your earliest convenience.

Our service area covers a large territory and as our business grows, we plan to enroll the services of many more sitters. If your organization has anyone or knows anyone interested in working in their neighborhood area to care for pets, we would appreciate your referring them to us.

We thank you for your time and look forward to serving you and your pets in the near future!

Sincerely,

XYZ Pet Sitters, Inc.

Another good method for finding qualified staff members is to check veterinarians' offices, especially those located within the area in which you need additional help. Often veterinary technicians or office workers will be interested in pet sitting as a second source of income. With their veterinary hospital experience and an employer's recommendation, such people will most likely be good pet sitters.

When you've exhausted your sources of personal referrals, you may find that you'll need to advertise in your local newspaper under "Help Wanted." I remember being very uneasy at first about using this method. Fortunately, my worries have been unfounded, and I've had some very nice individuals apply for our openings. Of course, there have been a few less-than-desirable applicants, but I've found my instinct to be of benefit in weeding these people out. I know the type of person that I'm looking for to represent my business, and I can almost immediately tell if a candidate holds promise. With time and practice, you'll develop these skills as well. Below are some samples of ads that I've used in recruitment.

Regardless of how you find your pet sitters and how well you know them, always have job seekers complete application forms. It is best if they return forms to you directly so that you can discuss the position with them. Review these applications while they are there to answer any questions you may have, and so that you can get better acquainted. If after this initial interview you feel that they are well suited to be pet sitters, your next step is to check references thoroughly.

> *Note*: I know of a few business owners who require that each person answering a newspaper ad submit a resume. The rationale here is that if the person is professional and interested enough in your opening, he or she will willingly and promptly mail credentials to you. If the person isn't willing to meet this request, he or she is immediately disqualified. This is a good way to assess the good candidates from the bad and saves you interviewing time.

Regarding the all-important screening process, I require at least two personal and business letters of reference before permitting any candidates to join my company as pet sitters. (No matter how well

Sample Help-Wanted Ads

Perfect Part-Time Job!
Must Be Honest, Dependable,
Love Animals, Have Car and Enjoy
Public. Flexible Hours.
Serious Inquiries Call:

XYZ Pet Sitters
999-8877
March 3 and 4 from 2 - 4 p.m.

XYZ PET SITTERS has openings
in your neighborhood area! For info.,
call 999-8877 March 3 and 4, 2-4 p.m.

PET LOVERS!

Perfect part-time job. XYZ Pet Sitters, Inc., has openings in southwest, northwest & southeast areas of W-S/ Forsyth Co. Have fun and earn money caring for pets in your neighborhood. Must be at least 21 yrs., have exc. refs., love pets, have transp. & be available 7-9am and 5-7pm daily. Serious inquiries call 999-8877, 3-5pm Mon, Jan. 11 & Tues, Jan. 12.

I know them, policy is policy, and it's best to allow no exceptions to the rule.) You should also discuss screening applicants with the insurance agent who sold you your bond. Through experience with bonds, he or she may have required applications or suggestions to help you find trustworthy individuals for your organization. Before checking references on an applicant, make sure that you have his or her written permission. Many companies will not release information about a former employee without a signed authorization to do so.

There are some business owners in large metropolitan areas who conduct a **very** thorough investigation of each potential pet sitter. Besides the personal and business references, they check the applicant's driving record, credit history, and they also ascertain that there's no criminal record on file. Some business owners look these records up themselves, while others require that the applicant produce these records or hire a data collection service to conduct the various searches. Regardless of which checking methods you use, make every effort to learn as much about your applicants as possible. Due to the nature of pet sitting and the risks and liability involved, you need to feel very comfortable and confident about the character and abilities of your staff members.

Another requirement of my sitters is that they be at least twenty-one years old. By this age, people usually have a couple of years of work or college experience that add to their common sense and maturity. Customers seem to have more peace of mind in having an adult look after their pets and home than, for example, a high school student.

Although it has not been intentional, all but seven of over a hundred trained sitters I've worked with through the years have been female! I find this interesting. Perhaps the flexible schedule or nurturing aspect of pet sitting appeals more to women. But whatever the reasons, customers seem to feel more at ease about handing over their housekey to a female sitter. You may find this trend to be true for your business as well.

I have found that pet sitting appeals to teachers, nurses and graduate students as a job with flexible hours. I've also had several married couples, two mother and daughter teams, and sisters work for my company. These sitting duos have been extremely popular with our clientele. Evidently customers like the double dose of attention their pets receive from a team visit! I've also had several real estate agents come on board as pet sitters. The flexible hours worked well with their schedules and permitted them to earn additional money.

Your clients can also be an excellent source of pet sitters. I've obtained some of my best sitters this way. They used our service, were extremely pleased, and then called to see if we had job openings. I have such good luck with clients who become sitters that, whenever we need additional sitters, I advertise in our company newsletter that goes out to clients.

There are lots of great people out there who will do a first-rate job of pet sitting for you, so don't be nervous when it's time to expand your staff and delegate more sitting assignments. More than likely you'll have more applicants for pet-sitting positions than you have openings.

Don't forget professional courtesy once you've found your new pet sitters. It's my opinion that if someone has taken the time to complete an employment application and talk with you, the least you can do is mail a letter of explanation or rejection. Applicants are grateful for the notification, and this attention to detail speaks well for your company.

SITTER ORIENTATION

Whether it's one new pet sitter or an entire group, it's very important to train your sitters in an orientation session. You'll want them to understand your company's policies, procedures, and what you expect from them as members of your staff. The more informed your pet sitters are, the better job they'll do as representatives of your company.

A new pet sitter's attendance at an orientation session should be mandatory before going out on assignments. After this session, many of my pet sitters tell me that they had had no idea so much was involved in being a professional pet sitter. They are amazed and also appreciative of all the information conveyed during our training session. They are also surprised at the length of the session: from four to six hours, depending upon the number of questions raised and amount of discussion. To help you conduct your own training sessions, I'm including an overview of what takes place in mine. Keep in mind that this is only a suggestion of possible format and content. Depending upon your geographic location and climate, there may be some specialized services your company will want to provide, for example, pool cleaning, in addition to the more general services provided by a pet sitter. The basics follow and you can tailor your orientation to fit your business.

I begin each session with introductions and then hand out folders of supplies (service contracts, business brochures and cards, notepads, key tags, self-addressed envelopes, etc.) that the pet sitters will use when working. I explain that the purpose of our training session is not to scare new pet sitters with all the things that *could* go wrong in the course of business, but, instead, to prepare them to avoid any problems, or to know how to handle them should they arise. I want my sitters always to be thinking and using their common sense.

After presenting some history on our company and the pet-

sitting industry itself, I discuss certain company formalities that include the following:

- COMPENSATION—when and how much the sitter is paid
- INSURANCE COVERAGE—the kind our company carries
- NON-COMPETITION CLAUSE—that is solely for my protection. (After all the time, effort, money and headaches I have expended with my pet-sitting business, the last thing I want is one of my sitters becoming my competition.) If you wish to require this signed statement from your pet sitters, be sure to consult an attorney about it. In some states, such a document won't hold up in court, or it may have to be meticulously worded in order to be worth the paper it's written on.

I next show a training video I've produced, "The New Pet Sitter." The video takes a new sitter step-by-step through an actual pet-sitting visit. A recent addition to my training program, the video is great not only because it's effective, but because it allows me to take a break and rest my voice for a few minutes. I highly recommend the video, but if it's not a possibility for you at this point, you can easily explain the ins and outs of pet sitting to your staff.

During this orientation, there are some points you should stress to new pet sitters. These include the following:

- Emphasize the importance of confidentiality of customers' names. One never knows who may overhear one's conversation as one describes the gorgeous art, coin or gun collection in the Smith's home. . . . Customers' names and the contents of their homes should remain confidential; letting their absence be known could invite a burglary. Coding housekeys anonymously is important in the event keys are ever lost or stolen. I instruct my sitters to code them by visit or stop (for example, #1, 2, 3, etc.). That way, only the sitter knows to which house they belong. Make your customers aware of their anonymity; this gives them peace of mind while they are away.
- An introductory meeting with the client and his or her pet(s) is an absolute must, unless extenuating circumstances pre-

clude it. This is normally a twenty- to thirty-minute visit that allows the client time to fill out your service contract and gives the sitter a chance to become acquainted with the pets and their routine. The meeting helps to ensure that a client feels comfortable since he or she knows the person who will have responsibility for his or her pet and home. Likewise, it also ensures that the sitter knows that the assignment is one he or she feels comfortable in accepting. It's an eerie feeling walking into a stranger's home and dealing with a pet you've never met before. All in all, an initial interview is highly recommended.

- Returning clients' housekeys can be handled in different ways. Some customers prefer the key left in their home on the final visit. Others want it held by the sitter and returned in person, just in case the owner is not able to return when planned. Many people these days have deadbolt locks for which a key is necessary to lock the door; therefore the key has to be returned in person. (In such instances, you may want to charge extra for the sitter's time and gasoline in returning the key, unless you've already allowed for this when setting your fees.) Many of our regular customers ask that the sitter keep their key and be on call as needed. This is nice as it shows one's services are well liked, and it also cuts down on time and gasoline spent in key pickups. In any event, you'll need to inform your new pet sitters of the various modes of key return, unless your company has a single procedure for this.

- Undoubtedly you have put thought and research into setting fees for your pet-sitting services. Thoroughly explain your pricing during orientation and spell out what the customer receives for this fee. Although you or whoever answers your business phone will usually quote prices for services, sitters should understand how to calculate fees and be able to respond intelligently to routine inquiries about prices.

- Discuss your company's payment policy. Will clients pay their sitter directly and trust that payment will be forwarded to the company, or will clients mail payment to your office?

Will major credit cards be accepted and, if so, how will this be handled? Are sitters allowed to accept tips and, if so, must they report them for proper taxation by your company? And do they keep the entire tip, or split it with the company? This is an important area that requires serious attention so as to avoid any confusion or misunderstanding in the future.

Note: Speaking of tips, inform new sitters not to be surprised at customers who remember their pet sitter with a souvenir or gift from their travels. Point out how good you feel to make rounds to a home during holidays and find a Christmas gift, or Valentine's box of candy, for YOU from "Muffin" or "Snowball" or "Fluffy." These thoughtful little remembrances from customers can make your day.

- Since driving is such an important aspect of pet sitting, stress to your sitters the need for careful driving habits at all times. The last thing you want is a speed demon representing your organization. Also, a clean car speaks well for the integrity of your pet sitters.

Note: For your own peace of mind, you may want to obtain an umbrella automobile insurance rider for your business. (This coverage was mentioned earlier under "Insurance" but deserves repeating.) If one of your sitters has an automobile accident while

pet sitting and expenses exceed the limitations of his or her car insurance, then your business policy would afford additional coverage. Discuss this with your insurance agent.

- Go over any equipment or supplies that you require or recommend during pet sitting. I remember when I first opened my pet-sitting business, I tried to think of EVERYTHING I might possibly need in the course of pet sitting. I bought so much—paper towels, garbage bags, pooper scoopers, flashlight, whisk broom, etc.—that I had to carry a huge bag to make rounds. What I quickly learned was that people who have pets have the items necessary to do a good job in caring for their pets. Now, the only items I suggest that my sitters invest in are the following:

  - CLIPBOARD—to hold service contracts so the customer has a hard surface to press on when filling it out. While the customer completes the contract during the initial interview, the sitter is free to get acquainted with the pets in the household.
  - KEY RETRIEVER—some type is absolutely MANDATORY, whether it's a string tied around a wrist or a belt clip-on type. There is nothing more horrifying than to have the wind blow the door shut (and locked) while the sitter is outside with the pet, and the key is on the kitchen counter. This is not only embarrassing, but it can be time-consuming and expensive if a

locksmith is required to get the sitter back into the house. So, stress to your sitters the importance of keeping housekeys attached to their persons while making pet-sitting rounds. I have tried all types of key retrievers and find the elasticized plastic wristbands are preferred by me and my sitters.

- CITY MAP—helpful for shortcuts and finding those streets when you thought you knew where you were going.
- SCHEDULE BOOK—whether it's a datebook or simply a monthly calendar, this is absolutely necessary for keeping up with pet-sitting visits, initial interview appointments and staff meetings. Not to mention all the other things one may need to remember in this busy day and age. WRITE IT DOWN so you don't find yourself needing to be in two places at the same time.
- FLASHLIGHT—this can be a very useful item when pet sitting. It can help you let yourself into a dark home, find an elusive cat that hides in nooks and crannies, and can serve as a weapon if need be (the battery-filled handle can pack a powerful punch should you ever need to defend yourself with it).
- LEASH—although clients should always provide one to use in walking their dog(s), sometimes they forget to leave it where you can find it. Or a worn leash could break from the strain of an energetic dog. Having a back-up leash may prove very handy.
- FLEA REPELLENT—this is a necessity for the occasional home that's filled with fleas. You don't want to carry the fleas into the home of another client or back to your own home. Nor do you want to be "eaten alive" while caring for the household pets. So invest in a good flea repellent.

- Discuss the type of notice you'll expect from sitters for vacation, illness and even resignation. You will need advance warning in order to schedule assignments and guarantee services to clients. Requiring a week's notice from sitters is reasonable; sitters usually know of upcoming vacations, engagements or exams. Of course, you can never plan on the flu, so in the event of a sitter's illness, have a back-up plan, or you'll find yourself scrambling at the last minute to feed hungry pets.

Other good information to share during a training session includes the following items.

- Insist that your sitters recognize and take advantage of free advertising at every opportunity. Advertising is expensive and sometimes beyond the reach of the small business—yet it's vital to any new business. There are many ways to spread the word about your services, though, with little or no expense. Ask sitters always to carry business cards and/or brochures and post them on bulletin boards in public places. Leave these items in a variety of business establishments and hand them out at social and civic gatherings. When shopping, give business cards to sales clerks. Give thought to places and people you may have never considered before; even those who may not have a pet probably know people who do and who may need your services. Word of mouth is often the best form of advertising for a service business, so do all you can to get the grapevine buzzing in many directions.
- Suggest that your sitters study literature from your office library or visit the local public library to familiarize themselves with the various types and breeds of dogs, cats and other household pets. Clients are always impressed when a pet sitter is knowledgeable about their particular pet.
- Tell your sitters the name of your insurance company and your agent's name. Discuss with them what your insurance covers, stressing the need for their conscientiousness while pet sitting. I give each of my sitters a letterhead form, signed by my insurance agent, that states and explains the types of insurance coverage carried by my business. This is proof of our coverage should a customer ever request it.
- A true sign of a conscientious, professional pet sitter is a daily note or log left in the customer's home. This may state the time of the visit, how the sitter found the pets and home upon each visit, weather conditions, etc. I furnish notepads for this but insist a note be left on whatever paper is available. Customers have raved about these notes and have said they enjoyed reading them very much. The daily record gave them assurance the sitter was there and made them feel as if they hadn't really been away. Some sitters are brief in

their notations, and others write essays on the antics of the pets. The notes come in handy should a customer return early and wonder if the sitter has already fed the pet(s) that day. Also, if a pet acts peculiarly, the sitter can make daily notes to cue the owner in to a potential problem. If a problem has occurred, the sitter can explain in the daily note what has transpired. Otherwise, the customer may wonder what took place in his or her absence. The daily notes are a very important part of your service. If pet sitters are doing a good job, the customer should not be able to tell the sitter has been around—except for the daily note.

- You'll want to know if customers are pleased with your services. A good way to get feedback is to have sitters leave some kind of evaluation form. Discuss the importance of this form with your new sitters. You or your sitter may also want to provide a self-addressed envelope with the evaluation form to encourage customers to return the form (and their payment!) to you. A rating form gives you valuable information based on customers' comments, suggestions and even constructive criticism. You can also use it to find out how they heard about your services to assess what form of advertising is working for your business.

- Returning customer calls promptly is a must for you and your sitters in creating a professional, positive image for your business. If it takes three days to return a call, a customer may wonder if your delivery of services is also haphazard. Even if customers are not leaving town for several weeks, they still appreciate speaking with their sitter and knowing they can count on the prompt professional services of this individual. After talking with their sitter and being assured of services, customers are relieved and feel secure in making flight or travel reservations. So always insist sitters call and introduce themselves to their customers as soon as possible—and preferably within twenty-four hours of the client's call to book pet-sitting services.

- First appearances do make strong impressions upon people, so remind your sitters of this and request that they be neat

and clean when going to an initial interview. To project a professional image, sitters should not smoke, chew gum or accept an alcoholic beverage in the course of an interview. Smoking can plant the fear of a house fire in customers, while accepting an alcoholic beverage can create fears of raids on their liquor cabinet. So, even though pet sitting is very informal, it is best to forego any of these activities as they reflect negatively on your professional image. Besides, the duration of house visits for interviews and service rounds is not that lengthy. Insist that your pet sitters refrain from smoking, drinking alcohol or chewing gum while on duty.

- Taking the garbage out on a final visit to a customer's home is a nice touch and speaks well for the thoroughness of your services. Empty cans of pet food in the trash tend to smell as they accumulate. Depositing the trash in an outside container results in a more pleasant return for your customer.

If your customer is away for an extended length of time, the sitter may need to take the trash out more often.

- Advise new pet sitters never to let a client leave a key hidden outside for them. Clients are notorious for leaving town in a hurry and forgetting this all-important task. An extra key can be made for a very small charge and given to the pet sitter, but a locksmith can be expensive, not to mention the extra time and headache this will entail. Also, don't agree to let clients drop their housekeys in the pet sitter's mailbox. Mail carriers have been known to pick up these keys (or envelopes with keys in them) and assume they are to be conveyed through the postal system.

- If pet sitters are to leave a self-addressed envelope for the client (to pay the bill and/or return your evaluation form), encourage them to provide *business-sized* envelopes. Clients don't like to fold their checks or forms origami style to fit small envelopes!

- If a sitter learns about the death of a client's pet, he or she should let your office know. Then you can change your records accordingly and send a sympathy card or remembrance to the client.

- Remind new pet sitters that feces should always be disposed of in a sanitary manner. Insist that the client or sitter provide plastic bags for this phase of cleanup.

- Tell sitters always to try contacting their absent clients should a disaster occur in your area. If there is an earthquake, tornado or hurricane, clients will most likely hear of it through the media and worry about the safety of their home and pets. The sitter should call the client promptly and give as much information as possible.
- If you've not already mailed a new client a brochure describing your services, request that your sitters leave one during their initial meeting. The fact that you have printed literature creates a more professional image for your business, so take advantage of it.
- By requiring a certain amount of notice from clients prior to their departure, you should have ample time to arrange for an initial interview with their sitter. However, clients will have emergencies due to illness or death and need to leave immediately, without meeting the sitter. Discuss these emergency situations with new pet sitters and your company's policy in handling them.
- Spend some time discussing how emergency pet-sitting situations should be handled. Should sitters contact you at home, call another staff member or handle the problem as they deem best? Prepare your new pet sitters with a plan of action for emergencies so that they won't panic should one occur.
- Get emergency numbers from your new sitters. If a sitter becomes sick or injured while pet sitting, you'll need to know whom to notify. Or, should you be unsuccessful in contacting one of your staff members, you may need to check with this emergency contact to ascertain the well-being and whereabouts of your pet sitter.
- More than likely, the insurance and bond coverage you purchase for your business will only cover sitters themselves in the course of pet-sitting duties. Stress to your sitters that for this reason, among others, they should go ALONE when making pet-sitting rounds. The customer has authorized only the sitter or your company's representative to have access to his or her home and pets. Should children accompany a

sitter, there is definitely a risk for something to go wrong or get broken. Should an adult friend or family member accompany a sitter and even sit in the car, neighbors may be watching and later exaggerate the scene by describing "a carload of people" who showed up to care for the pets. To avoid any unnecessary problems, the sitter should always work alone. If a sitter requires assistance with an assignment, then you will need to intervene, making your client aware of any problems and the reason additional people needed to enter his or her home.

- A final word of advice you could offer is to encourage your new pet sitters to conduct business by the Golden Rule. Treating each customer, pet and home as they would their own will surely minimize the potential for problems and pave their path to success.

The next part of my orientation and training session for sitters involves going over the various literature and business forms my service uses. These are found in the information packets mentioned at the beginning of this chapter. Although some of the forms are self-explanatory, I still go over each one. I want to make sure that new pet sitters understand the reason for each piece of printed material and that they know how and when to use it. Since you'll want your new pet sitters to be thoroughly informed, I suggest you devote some time to form and literature explanation in your training sessions.

Although pet sitters are not expected to be roving veterinarians, a good pet sitter should be able to recognize the symptoms of illness in a pet and have some knowledge of first aid if a pet becomes injured while under your company's care. I know of a few pet-sitting services that require their new sitters to volunteer several hours at a local veterinarian's office, thereby gaining valuable expertise in dealing with sick or injured animals. This is an excellent idea in several respects and one that you'll surely want to consider.

Another way of approaching first aid in your training sessions is to show videos that deal with the subject. While these were not available when I first began to expand my staff, now there are a few good ones on the market. If the cost of videos is prohibitive for your business, you should consider investing in an office library of first aid and pet care books, which new sitters may borrow to read. Or, given the low cost of some of these books, you might give each new pet sitter a paperback book on general first aid for pets. Or you could require that sitters purchase a copy as an integral part of their supplies.

After a final question and answer period, I conclude my training sessions with a pop quiz. This is a multiple choice test that includes questions from all the areas addressed in our orientation. The test allows me to see which new pet sitters have a complete understanding of what pet sitting entails and how our company policies and procedures work. By the test scores, I can see which areas might need further clarification or which attendee was sleeping during the training program. (Anyone napping during the session can be immediately disqualified from joining our staff!) An additional benefit of the test is that clients are always impressed when they learn that my pet sitters are not only trained, but they are tested as well. Thoroughness in training heightens our level of professionalism and increases our credibility. Make every effort to get your new pet sitters off on the right track. This initial training will pay off in the long run.

MANAGING AND MOTIVATING SITTERS

Starting your own pet-sitting service may present you with your first experience in managing employees, and you may need some assistance or reassurance in this area. First of all, remember that a pet-sitting business is somewhat nontraditional as compared to other business environments. After you've recruited and trained your staff members, you'll probably find that you communicate mainly by phone and rarely see them. That's why I feel that pet sitting is one of the few businesses that still thrives on the old-fashioned element of trust. There must be trust between the client and the pet sitter, as there must be trust between the pet sitter and the employer. You won't be able to follow your pet sitters and check on the jobs they do for you; you'll have to trust that they will satisfactorily fulfill their job obligations. You will also need to trust that clients will let you know if they are displeased with your company's services.

That's why it's important to use some type of client evaluation form or call your clients for feedback about your sitters and services. Then share this information with the sitters. If they are doing a terrific job, tell them, praise them, commend them! Let them know how much you appreciate their efforts. Likewise, if there's any type of complaint or dissatisfaction, constructively discuss this with the sitter. Then put your discussion and the outcome of it in writing and file it in the sitter's personnel file. Should the same complaint be voiced again about the pet sitter, you'll have good documentation for supporting whatever disciplinary action you decide to take. But hopefully, if you've gone to the trouble of finding good pet sitters, you'll be singing their praises instead of disciplining them.

> *Note*: Since you will see your staff infrequently, consider taking or requesting their photos for display on your office bulletin board. This allows you or your office staff to put faces with names and personalizes your operations a little more. You'll also be able to give a physical description of the pet sitter if requested (for purposes of identification) by a client.

Pet sitting is also different from other more traditional businesses in that it usually requires part-time or "split-shift" employees who work on call, usually with no guaranteed paycheck and minimal, if any, benefits. The work can be demanding, with weekends and holidays often the busiest times and, as with any job, burnout has to be guarded against. To do this, make sure your pet sitters have an occasional weekend or holiday off. Keep enough pet sitters on staff or back-ups available so that you're not too dependent on any one sitter. If you started your pet-sitting business by making all the visits yourself, remember what some of the jobs and some of the clients can be like—and be considerate of your staff members! If you're good to your employees, they'll be good to you.

Experience has also shown that most people who want to be pet sitters do so because of a genuine love of animals and the appealing nature of the flexible hours and independent work. It has been said that nursing or teaching takes a special kind of person, and I've found this to be true of pet sitting as well. But, as in any profession, some inspiration is nice and necessary to keep these "naturals" motivated and eager to do a good job for your company. Some ways to motivate your pet sitters include the following ideas:

- Institute a sliding scale of compensation. In other words, give your pet sitters some economic incentive! Give small pay increases after every three or six months of service with your company, or whatever you feel comfortable with.
- Hold sitter contests. Give prizes or cash awards for the sitter who sits for the most clients each month, brings in the most new business each quarter, or who receives the best evaluation forms from clients each month.
- Give a yearly Christmas or appreciation bonus to sitters who've done an outstanding job during the year. Sometimes the gesture and recognition mean more to employees than the actual amount of the bonus.
- Send out monthly letters to staff members. Tell them of any new business policies or procedures. Inform them of any

discounts on services you're now offering. Introduce new staff members. Commend pet sitters who've done an exemplary job. Announce winners of contests. Use the letters to keep sitters informed and motivated.

- Charge a holiday surcharge for visits made on certain nationally recognized holidays. Give the surcharge to the pet sitter as a bonus for working during these periods.
- Give pet sitters reduced fees on pet-sitting services from your company.

STAFF MEETINGS

Regularly held staff meetings are important to keep your staff informed and can also be a good motivator. They allow you to personally interact and communicate, and they also allow your sitters the opportunity to meet one another and compare sitting experiences and knowledge.

I like to make my meetings educational as well by inviting a guest speaker who can talk about something that will be helpful to my staff members. We've had presentations from veterinarians, karate experts, pet photographers, kennel club spokespeople, humane society personnel, and even a tax accountant. During one get-together we saw a video, and at another we addressed post cards for a direct mailing. Several sitters have gotten to know each other well from these meetings and become good friends. The camaraderie is always enjoyable and somewhat motivational, and I think the refreshments I provide are a way of saying "thank you" to the sitters for the terrific job they do.

Consider having these meetings as your budget allows. Hold them in your home and make them potluck if nothing else! It's the sharing of information that will count and benefit your sitters. Plus, it's impressive to clients when they learn that these meetings are held on a regular basis and that education is ongoing for your staff members.

5

Advertising

THE IMPORTANCE OF A BROCHURE

Your office is organized, your staff trained, your insurance and bond are in effect, and you're ready to begin pet sitting. How do you get that phone ringing with customers requesting your services? You've got to get the word out about your business and seize every opportunity to educate the public about the valuable in-home pet care you provide.

Advertising is a critical factor in the success of your business. After all, people won't patronize your business if they aren't aware that it exists. I think this is where I made a mistake when I opened my pet-sitting business in 1983. I began my business on such a shoestring budget that there was little left over for advertising. Had I spent more on my initial advertising and reached more people, I'm sure my business would have grown much faster. There is much to be said for the old adage that you've got to spend money to make money. So, when planning your operating budget, be sure to allot an adequate figure for advertising, especially during your first few years of operation.

Unfortunately, the usual forms of advertising (television, radio, magazine, newspaper and billboard) can be overwhelmingly expensive for the small business just getting started. However, through years of experience I've discovered there are many ways to advertise your pet-sitting service that can be very effective and involve only a minimal cost. Let's discuss these inexpensive advertising techniques first, as a penny saved is a penny earned.

To start, have a nicely printed brochure describing your pet-sitting service. Your brochures and business cards will come in handy time and time again in promoting your service. Often, they'll create the first impression of your business so it's important that these materials be well written, attractive and indicative of your professionalism.

If graphic design is not your area of expertise, hire someone in this field to help you create this literature for your service. There are many freelancers who may do a good job but charge less than an established advertising or public relations agency. Again, interview prospective candidates for experience and credentials and shop around for the best deal.

A good brochure should contain information about what your service provides, the advantages it offers, how it works and, probably, how much it costs. You may also want to include some background material about yourself and/or your pet sitters, relating why

you started the business, your past experience, and the number of pets in your own household. You'll definitely want your company logo and phone number prominently displayed, and you may want to include a photo of yourself and/or your staff members. Although there will be an initial expense for the writing and layout of your brochure, it will be money well spent. You'll then have a nice brochure representing your business, which you can proudly use for years to come.

> *Note*: An added bonus to a well-designed brochure is that you can often take a particular portion of it—for example, the front section—and have it enlarged for use as a flyer or small poster. Keep this idea in mind when preparing your business literature so as to get the most mileage out of your advertising budget.

Once you have your brochures, flyers and business cards, here are some ways they can be used to advertise your services:

1) GROOMING SHOPS, VETERINARY OFFICES, PET SHOPS—Go where the pets are and introduce yourself to the management. Ask for a moment of their time to explain your pet-sitting service and then ask if you may leave your brochures and business cards in a conspicuous location.

    Note: Don't be afraid to approach veterinarians who offer boarding facilities for pets. Although you are each other's competition, hopefully, you can establish a harmonious relationship. There will be times when boarding facilities will be completely booked and a veterinarian may refer customers to you. Sometimes vets recommend older pets be left at home and, again, refer customers to you. Likewise, there may be a time when you are completely booked or feel a pet needs more medical attention than you feel comfortable providing. A cooperative relationship with local veterinarians and boarding kennels can be very beneficial for all concerned, including the pets and their owners. It also speaks well for your professional maturity.

2) TRAVEL AGENCIES—Visit or write all the travel agencies in your community informing them of your services. Supply them with your brochures and business cards. This is

(continued on page 73)

VACATION TRAVEL??

You can trust your pet to us.

XYZ Pet Sitters, Inc.

- personalized, loving in-home pet care

- make your home look "lived in"

- reasonable rates

- four (4) days notice required

- service available in 27103, 27104, 27106 areas of Winston-Salem

Since 1983
Winston-Salem, NC
999-8877

XYZ Pet Sitters, Inc.

— Bonded —   — Insured —

Travel Agency Letter

Dear employees of Vacation Travel Agency:

Enclosed is information describing our personalized home pet care service, XYZ Pet Sitters, Inc. We would appreciate it if you would circulate or post our brochure within your office. Our service may make traveling much easier for many of your clients!

We are happy to provide you with additional brochures upon request. We look forward to serving you and your customers and appreciate any referrals.

Sincerely yours,

XYZ Pet Sitters, Inc.

Sample Promotion Letter

XYZ Pet Sitters, Inc.   Telephone 999-8877
123 Any Street
Anywhere, U.S.A. 20002

During the months of April, May and June, XYZ Pet Sitters, Inc., is having a special promotional campaign in which we invite your travel agents to participate. We have been providing the best in personalized home pet care to area residents faced with traveling since 1983. In an effort to increase our business, we are offering the following promotion to local travel agents since you know best who may be in need of our services.

* a $5.00 "commission" for each new customer you refer to us who books our services for a minimum of 3 visits. This $5.00 referral fee will be paid the first of each month (May, June and July) directly to the agent responsible for sending the new client to us.

* a 10% introductory discount will be extended to your clients who use our services as a result of your referral (new clients only).

Brochures describing our services and discount coupons (which the referring agent will sign) will be provided by XYZ Pet Sitters, Inc., for your use during this promotional campaign. Their size allows them to easily fit inside the jackets of airline tickets, business envelopes, etc. Your participation could include asking your clients if they have pets that will need to be cared for, or simply just inserting literature about our services in your mail outs. You determine how actively you participate in our promotional campaign!

I hope that you will take part in the promotion since we all can benefit from it. Your agents can earn extra cash, your clients will appreciate the discount extended through your agency, and our list of satisfied customers will grow.

Please call me at 999-8877 by April 3, 1989, if you wish to participate in this campaign and we'll get brochures and coupons to you promptly. I look forward to working with you this spring!

Very truly yours,

Patti J. Moran
President

COUPON

XYZ Pet Sitters, Inc.

XYZ Pet Sitters, Inc. is pleased to extend a 10% introductory discount to clients of _____ .
This coupon must be presented when a house key is picked up by XYZ Pet Sitters, Inc., and is valid only for services consisting of 3 or more visits per home.

Expires 6/30/89   _____
                                Travel Agent

COUPON

AD SAMPLES

an excellent resource for reaching people who will be traveling. A sample letter appears on page 70.

3) HUMANE SOCIETY, KENNEL CLUB, CAT ASSOCIATIONS— Write to these organizations, enclosing your brochures and business cards. Offer a free pet-sitting visit to anyone adopting a pet through your local Humane Society, or offer kennel club members an introductory discount on their first use of your services. These are important groups to notify about your business; the chances are great that individuals associated with them are true animal lovers who most likely may need your service at some time. The sample body of a notification letter is shown in Chapter 4, ''Personnel.''

4) NEWCOMERS TO YOUR AREA—These are people you continually want to reach since they probably don't know their neighbors well enough to impose on them to look after their pets. ''Home'' is probably somewhere else, so many newcomers will most likely travel for holidays, etc. How do you reach them? Write to your local **Chamber of Commerce** informing the organization about your business (or consider joining the Chamber of Commerce if the benefits are worth the annual membership dues). Contact your local **Welcome Wagon** or similar organization with information on your services. Mail your brochure to all the **Real Estate Agencies** in your community. They sell homes to newcomers every day! Also, a growing service in many communities makes moving easy by seeing that utilities are hooked up and turned on for newcomers. If such a service exists in your area, ask the people if they would tell newcomers with pets about your business. I know of one pet sitter who learns about newcomers by checking the water connections, which are public city records. Regardless of how you find newcomers, don't miss out on the business they can provide. And once you've determined who they are, try sending them a welcoming letter that, of course, introduces your service. A sample follows:

Newcomer Letter

Dear Newcomer:

Welcome to your new home! We hope that you will enjoy our city and all that it has to offer. As lifelong residents of the area, we can truly say that this is a great place to live and work. We hope you'll soon agree.

In the event that you are a pet owner or a potential pet owner, we wanted to make you aware of XYZ Pet Sitters, Inc. We have found that new residents face a problem with what to do with their pet when traveling on business or pleasure. Often, there is no family close by to call on, and neighbors take a while to get to know. In any event, we wanted to make you aware of our service and hope you'll take the time to read the enclosed brochure, which explains our business in more detail. You can rest assured that each staff member is bonded and insured.

Again, welcome to the area. Please call us if we may be of service to you.

Sincerely,

XYZ Pet Sitters, Inc.

5) HOUSECLEANING AND LAWN CARE SERVICES—Using the Yellow Pages of your telephone directory, write to all of these types of services with information about your pet-sitting business. The people doing this type of work visit homes every day; they notice pets and can spread word of your services or leave a brochure for their clients. You could also ask if they would include your brochure with their next billing, or if they would sell you their mailing list. You may have to offer something (money, discounts, reciprocal referrals) in return for this help in advertising

Real Estate Company Letter

Dear employees of ABC Realtors:

Enclosed is our brochure describing our services to the community. I think we may be of service to you while you are taking vacation, business trips or working overtime. Your clients who own pets also may find our services of special interest. We would appreciate it if you could circulate or post our brochure within your company.

Please keep our service in mind as you sell real estate to newcomers to our area who are pet owners. We would be happy to provide you with additional brochures upon request.

Thank you for your time and consideration.

Sincerely yours,

XYZ Pet Sitters, Inc.

your business. But some may remember what it was like when they started out and sympathetically give your service a plug!

6) GARDEN CLUBS—Obtain a list of the garden clubs in your service area and write to them, enclosing your brochure. Even if club members don't have pets, they probably have plants that need water and care when they're away from home. Remember that anyone who hears about your service may tell someone else, creating a grapevine effect. This is how you can inexpensively get the word out that you're in business. A sample of this type of letter is shown on page 76.

7) LAW ENFORCEMENT AGENCIES—It is a smart business practice to inform your local police and sheriff's department of the valuable crime deterrence your service pro-

vides. If your community has a Crime Stop or Neighborhood Watch program, law enforcement personnel may
spread the word about your services. And, heaven forbid,
should you find one of your homes has been burglarized,
the law enforcement officials you contact will already be
familiar with your business. A sample of the letter that I
use to inform law enforcement officials about my new
business is shown opposite.

8) FRIENDS AND FAMILY MEMBERS—Get your brochures to
those who know you and will support you in your new
venture. With an estimated 60 percent of American house-
holds owning some type of pet, everybody knows or works
with someone who has a pet, and that someone may be
interested in using your services. A personal recommendation also means a lot in this business, so get your friends
and family members to spread the word about your unique
service.

9) LOCAL BUSINESSES AND COMPANIES—Obtain a list from
your local Chamber of Commerce of the major employers
in your area. Then send your brochure to the personnel

Garden Club Sample Letter

Dear Maple Leaf Garden Club:

Enclosed you will find brochures describing services
provided by XYZ Pet Sitters, Inc. Although our primary
function is personalized home pet care while the owner
is away, we are also happy to provide loving care for
your plants. Prices are based on travel and time involved; however, we are reasonable!

We are a locally owned and operated business, and we
are bonded and insured. We would appreciate so much
your announcing our service at your next club meeting.
We hope we may be of service to your members in the
near future.

Sincerely yours,

XYZ Pet Sitters, Inc.

Law Enforcement Introduction Letter

XYZ PET SITTERS, INC.
123 Any Street
Anywhere, U. S. A. 20002
(909) 999-8877

Dear Chief ————————:

Enclosed you will find information describing XYZ Pet Sitters, Inc. Our service involves going into customers' homes to care for their pets while they are away on vacation, business, etc. We feel that an important part of our service is giving the home a "lived-in" look by bringing in mail and newspapers, opening and closing curtains and alternating lights—all measures which we hope will be crime deterrents. Although we certainly hope we never encounter a home that has been burglarized, in the event that we do, our staff has been instructed to leave the premises immediately and contact the appropriate law enforcement officials.

As spring and summer approach, we anticipate being very busy in the city and county area. For this reason, we wanted to make you and your department aware of our service and our sincere desire to have a good working relationship with the police department. If our brochures can be incorporated into any of the Community Watch or Crimestoppers programs, we will be happy to supply literature or assist in any way that we can.

Each of our pet sitters is bonded, insured, reliable, responsible and hard working.

We appreciate the fine efforts of your department and thank you for notifying your staff that our service is available.

Should you or your departmental members have any further questions regarding XYZ Pet Sitters, Inc., please give us a call.

Sincerely yours,

XYZ Pet Sitters, Inc.

departments of these companies. Often benefits managers in these departments are on the lookout for services and information that will be useful to their employees. They may print a blurb about your service in their company newsletter, or post your brochure on employee bulletin boards or in the company cafeteria. Consider offering their employees an introductory discount for a limited time to make such publicity efforts worthwhile. A copy of the letter I send to corporations is shown below.

Company Business Letter

Dear employees of Atlas Law Offices:

Enclosed is our brochure describing how we can be of service to you while you are taking vacation, business trips or working overtime.

We would appreciate it if you would circulate or post our brochure on an employee bulletin board or mention us in your company newsletter. Please call if you need more information or additional brochures.

Thank you for your time and consideration.

Sincerely yours,

XYZ Pet Sitters, Inc.

---

10) CIVIC CLUBS AND NONPROFIT ORGANIZATIONS—Obtain a list of these from your local Chamber of Commerce and, again, send your brochure and introductory letter to each organization. By offering members an introductory discount, you may encourage them to announce your letter and circulate your brochure at their next meeting. Also, if you're comfortable with public speaking, offer to give a talk about your new business at their club's next meeting. Guest speakers are often in demand, and you'll find most

audiences interested in your talk and appreciative of your visit. Plus, after meeting you personally, some group members will feel confident about giving your service a try. If just the thought of public speaking gets your knees shaking, remember that most people share this fear to some degree. The fact that you're willing to get up and talk about your business will be admired and, after a few speeches, you'll be a lot more at ease with making public presentations. A sample of an introductory letter is shown below.

Civic Clubs and Organizations Letter

Dear Arts Council members:

Enclosed you will find our brochure, which describes the services of XYZ Pet Sitters, Inc. We have been caring for pets in the area since 1983.

We are trying to reach all pet owners in the community before the summer vacation season begins. We would appreciate so much your circulation of our brochure at your next meeting. Any member of your organization using our service for the first time before_____ will receive a 10% discount on our services. (They must identify themselves as a member.)

Please call if you need more brochures or if we can provide additional information.

Sincerely yours,

XYZ Pet Sitters, Inc.

---

11) APARTMENT COMPLEXES—Using the Yellow Pages of your telephone directory, call all apartment complexes in your service area to determine which ones allow pets. Then, send your brochure to the apartment managers of these complexes and ask that they inform resident pet owners

of your services. Many apartment complexes provide a welcome packet of information to new residents, and your brochure may be added. Inquire about this possibility. Below is a copy of the letter that I have mailed to apartment complex managers.

Apartment Complex Letter

Dear Manager of Cross Creek Apartments:

Enclosed is our brochure describing the services of XYZ Pet Sitters, Inc. We have been caring for area pets since 1983. Since your apartment complex allows pets, we would appreciate your posting our brochure in a conspicuous location. Please let me know if you would be interested in incorporating our brochure into your apartment's welcome material for new residents. I will be happy to provide you with additional brochures.

Thank you for spreading the word about our services. We look forward to caring for the pets at your apartment complex.

Sincerely yours,

XYZ Pet Sitters, Inc.

---

12) CONDOMINIUM COMPLEXES—Condominiums are springing up everywhere. My experience has shown that they appeal to young professionals who may travel a great deal in their occupations and may need your services. Most condominiums have a governing board made up of residents. Get your brochures to these board members for display in their clubhouse or inclusion in their resident newsletter.

Note: Do not go out and stuff brochures in mailboxes or doorways. Stuffing mailboxes (without postage and mail service) is a crime, and most apartments and condominiums adhere to a

strict no solicitation policy. You can create a negative image of your business by engaging in these practices.

13) BULLETIN BOARDS—You may not have noticed these before, but they are showing up in more and more places. Grocery stores, restaurants, laundromats and recreation facilities often have one available for public use. Start looking (and encourage your sitters to do so) and taking advantage of these to post your business card, brochure or flyer. It's a great form of free advertising!

14) LOCAL COLLEGES AND SCHOOLS—These institutions have employees and students (and bulletin boards) who are likely to be pet owners. Send your brochure to the Language, Anthropology, Archeology and Geography Departments (to name a few) at these schools. Professors often organize field trips, and someone in their group may be glad to hear of your services.

15) COMMUNITY GROUPS—Whether it's the YMCA, United Way, your local humane society or another charity, get involved. Represent your company by volunteer participation in your community. You'll not only benefit personally, but also get the word out about your business.

16) BUSINESS MEETINGS, SEMINARS, LECTURES—Seek out resources that are available in your community for the business owner. There are often lectures and workshops sponsored by the Chamber of Commerce, Small Business

Administration, Internal Revenue Service or professional groups that will help you in various aspects of running your business. These are sometimes free or offered at a nominal charge. They not only provide a learning experience, but are valuable networking sessions. You meet others in the business world and at the same time get to advertise your pet-sitting service.

17) CHURCH OR TEMPLE ACTIVITIES—Don't forget that church or temple socials, committee meetings and circle groups consist of people who could welcome the news of your pet-sitting services. Inform your congregation about your new business and ask for the support of the membership.

18) NEWS RELEASES—These can be worth their weight in gold with the free publicity they may generate for you. Write an informative news release about the opening of your pet-sitting service and mail it to local television and radio stations, and newspapers. Follow up with a phone call to determine if any of the media is interested in interviewing you about your new service from either a human interest or business angle. If they bite and put you on the local evening news, this is valuable free advertising most small business owners otherwise could rarely afford! Aggressively go after it. A sample of a news release is shown here.

News Release

Date: May 1, 1991	For Further
For: XYZ Pet Sitters, Inc.	Information Contact:
For Release: Immediately	Jane Smith, President

New Pet-Sitting Business Opens in Piedmont

Winston-Salem, N.C. . . . Area pet owners now have an alternate choice for pet care during vacations and business trips. Jane Smith, President, has opened XYZ Pet Sitters, Inc., at 123 Anywhere Street. The unique service provided by the company means that pet owners can now leave their household pet(s) in the comfort and familiarity of home.

"One of our insured and bonded staff members will visit a home on a daily basis to feed, water and care for the pet(s). And, most importantly, we'll provide lots of tender loving care and personalized attention during each visit," said Smith, President of the newly formed company.

XYZ Pet Sitters, Inc., has a staff of eight professional pet sitters, all of whom truly love pets and who have been thoroughly trained by the company. Not only do they look after the household pets in pampered style, but they also are happy to bring in newspapers, mail and even water houseplants. "We want every pet owner to be able to leave home with peace of mind, knowing his or her pet(s) and home are in our responsible care," notes Smith.

All clients making reservations for pet-sitting services during the month of May will receive a 10% discount off the total sitting fee. "This offer is to introduce our services to Piedmont pet owners and is a part of our grand opening celebration," said Smith. To get additional information or make a reservation, call XYZ Pet Sitters, Inc., at 999–8811.

---

19) DISCOUNTS—As mentioned earlier, offering discounts to employee groups or customers referred to you by dog groomers, travel agents, etc., can be a terrific form of advertising. It's especially helpful in encouraging new customers to give your service a try. As well as helping to get your business off the ground, discounts can also boost business during slow periods. Once customers have tried and been pleased with your services, you know they'll become repeat customers.

20) VISUAL PRESENTATIONS—Put together a slide show or short video presentation showing your services in action. Offer to show this program at Board of Realtor meetings, garden club meetings, travel fairs and other community events and meetings. Again, if you're inexperienced or uncomfortable with public speaking, now may be the time for you to overcome your fears for the sake of your business.

21) SATISFIED CUSTOMERS—The best form of advertising your business can have is the client who praises your services.

Sometimes a service business can be slow to grow because it often depends upon word-of-mouth recommendations to build clientele. Although word-of-mouth advertising may take longer to give your business a boost, it's still the greatest advertising around. To motivate clients to tell others about your business, try offering them a discount or gift certificate for each referral they send you. At the very least, send a thank you note for their recommendation of your service.

22) OPEN YOUR EYES—Watch not only for bulletin boards but also for pets. Keep your business cards and brochures with you at all times; you never know when you may need them. If I see a pet waiting in a car for its owner, I slip a brochure under the car's windshield wiper. If I see a pet owner out walking a dog, I stop and ask if they've heard of our pet-sitting service. Yes, some assertiveness is necessary in order to run a successful business. Take advantage of all free opportunities to inform the public about your pet sitting and suggest that your staff members do the same. One of my ingenious pet sitters has even started studying the shopping carts in line with her at the supermarket. If she spots pet food in the cart, she strikes up a conversation with that shopper and tells about our services.

23) PROMOTION AND NEW HIRE ANNOUNCEMENTS—Look for these in your local newspaper or business publications and newsletters. Send the people mentioned brochures and business cards, along with a personal note either congratulating their achievement or welcoming them to your community. End your note by saying that you hope they'll call if you can be of service to them when they travel.

24) SEIZE ALL FREE OPPORTUNITIES—And don't forget opportunity exists at cocktail parties, PTA meetings, diet groups, exercise classes, Christmas parades, craft shows, bowling leagues, day-care centers, etc. There are many pet owners out there, and you want to reach as many as possible.

As these twenty-four ideas illustrate, there are limitless ways to make the public aware of your new pet-sitting service. So, now that I've convinced you of the advertising value of a brochure, business card, business letterhead and postage stamp, let's move on to other advertising techniques.

INEXPENSIVE WAYS TO ADVERTISE

1) PLASTIC BADGES—Invest a few dollars in a plastic lapel badge that has your business name, logo and your name printed on it. WEAR IT ALL THE TIME! People read these, and you'll be amazed at the number of times people will inquire about your occupation. Store clerks, waiters and waitresses, post office personnel—these are just a few who have asked about my pet-sitting service simply from reading my badge.

   Note: Wear your badge when going to a customer's home for an initial interview. It lets the customer know who's at the door and presents an official and professional image for a sitter.

2) MAGNETIC CAR PLATES—These are a bit more expensive than plastic lapel badges, but well worth their cost in the advertising they generate for your business. My car signs

get so much attention and bring in so many new customers, I wish I had invested in them when first opening my business. I highly recommend you give this purchase top priority in your advertising budget. Shop around for the best price.

Note: When you're driving around town with your business signs for all the world to see, make sure you drive in a careful manner. As noted earlier, you don't want people associating XYZ Pet Sitters with speed demons.

Also, when making pet-sitting rounds, take the magnetic plates off of your car doors. Otherwise, your clients and their homes

will not remain confidential, as you have assured them they will be.

3) COSTUMES—Rent (or make) a cute animal costume and then walk city streets during lunch hours, handing out your brochures! A cute costumed ''animal'' (you or someone you've hired) may show up all kinds of places. Of course, you'll need to get permission for a costumed pet to appear, but investigate the possibilities of outdoor concerts, children's story hours at the library (parents go too), craft fairs, street festivals, dog and cat shows, etc. It's a relatively inexpensive and well-received means of advertising.

4) T-SHIRTS/SWEATSHIRTS—With the popularity of T-shirts and sweatshirts these days, a well-designed one will advertise your business for you! I've had numerous people stop me to inquire about our services after reading my shirt! They may also appeal to your customers and can be sold at a profit for your business. Shop around before placing an order; prices do vary. If you can't afford these initially, keep them in mind for purchase later on.

5) CITY OR COUNTY TAX OFFICE—Most counties require dog owners to list dogs they own and pay the appropriate tax assessed on these pets. Dog tags are issued to pet owners from this annual tax listing. You may be able to purchase (or copy) names and addresses of dog owners from your tax office's master list. You could then mail these pet owners information about your pet-sitting service. Time and money will be required to do a mass mailing of this sort, but it's a great way of directly reaching people who may need your services. Taking this idea a step further, you may include a presitting questionnaire with your mailing. This could be a post-card size form that dog owners could quickly fill out and mail back, indicating preliminary interest in your services. The business this mailing may generate could far exceed the costs involved.

6) PROGRAMS AND BULLETINS—Explore the many activities in your community that use printed programs with adver-

tising space. Some of these include: Little Theatre programs, high school sports programs, symphony sponsors, professional/minor league sports promotions, Junior League newsletters, ski or diving club bulletins and a host of others. Advertising on this smaller scale is generally cheaper than other media and gives you a known target group. You can also use these advertisements to offer introductory discounts to ski club members or, for example, to symphony season ticket holders.

7) POSTERS—These can also be helpful in getting the word out about your business. Since they are generally larger than the business flyer or brochure, they are more easily noticed on community bulletin boards. You may want to check into the cost of having some of these printed for your business.

8) SPECIALTY ITEMS—These include magnets, pens, pet food lids, key-chains and pet-theme calendars, to name a few. While such items are a good form of advertising, they become expensive when given out to the general public. My experience has shown that most pet sitters use the specialty items as a way to say "thank you" to their clients. They mail a calendar with an annual holiday card, or they leave a refrigerator magnet during the last visit of a sitting assignment. If you look into specialty items for your business, it's a good idea to shop around for the best price.

I have learned from the start that pet owners come in all shapes and sizes—from different economic levels and with a wide range of interests. So it's difficult to pinpoint one specific group for advertising purposes. The one thing they do have in common is a genuine love of their pets. Keep this in mind and try to reach all types of pet owners in your advertising efforts.

REACHING THE MASSES

The best way to reach a large number of people with your advertising message is through the newspaper or radio and television stations. However, these are usually the most expensive forms of advertising. My experiences and opinions about these three media follow.

NEWSPAPER—This advertising will get you results. But before you take out an expensive display ad, try these suggestions first. Send out the news release that was discussed in more detail earlier in this chapter. This is such a good idea that it's worth repeating. Deliver or mail your news release to the business editor of your local newspaper(s). The openings of new businesses are often considered newsworthy enough to rate a free paragraph on the business page. Some smaller or rural newspapers will even run a full-fledged article free, announcing the opening and details of your business. And, since pet sitting is a relatively new concept in many areas, your business will intrigue newspaper reporters. From a human interest standpoint, pet sitting has potential for a good story. Your service can be approached from the angle of its uniqueness, its potential to deter crime, or its female-ownership (if applicable). Call reporters assigned to human interest articles, as well as radio and television stations, to inquire if anyone would like to interview you for a story. If so, you're on your way. Often these stories do more to promote your business and lend credibility than any amount of paid advertising.

> *Note*: When possible, it's a good idea to check stories and articles before publication or broadcast. You want to ensure that your comments were not misconstrued, and that the story presents you and your business favorably.

In addition to any free media coverage you may receive, you will need to buy some advertising. An inexpensive form of newspaper advertising is to run a short classified ad about your service under the "Pets" heading. Readers scanning this column for a pet are apt to need your services one day. Some newspapers have a "Consumer Review" or "Business Review" section which, for a fee, will run an article and picture about your business. These are sometimes called advertorials. I have tried these several times and always receive an excellent response.

A small display ad with a catchy logo underneath, such as HOLIDAY TRAVEL? or BUSINESS TRAVEL? or GOING ON VACATION? will also get noticed. I have found advertising in Sunday through

Wednesday papers to get a better response than Thursday through Saturday, as those are the days people tend to travel and, therefore, miss the daily local newspaper. Advertising in the travel, entertainment and sports sections of the newspaper has also been effective. It can be costly, though, so I primarily advertise before holidays, during the summer vacation months, and on the anniversary date of my business opening. (Announcing the birthday or age of your business lends further credibility, as it shows you have staying power and are not a fly-by-night operation.)

Newspaper advertising does get noticed and creates name recognition with repetition. If the ad is distinctive, people will remember it long after the newspaper has been discarded.

> *Note*: If you operate your pet-sitting service in an extremely large city, newspaper advertising may not be the wisest use of your advertising dollar. For one thing, the cost may be prohibitive. Secondly, it may result in an annoying number of crank calls. Thirdly, you may not even cover the entire city with pet-sitting services. So, give careful thought before using any form of mass media advertising. And, when you do, be sure to specify city areas where pet-sitting services are available to make maximum use of your advertising dollar.

RADIO—I have mixed feelings about this form of advertising. Calls for our services did come in the days my radio commercials were broadcast. However, I'm not convinced that the business generated from the commercials paid for the high cost of airing them. Radio advertising is expensive for the small business owner; I recommend that you reserve its use until after you've gotten your business off the ground and have some advertising dollars to spare.

Should you decide to pursue radio advertising, keep the following in mind. First of all, do your homework by calling and researching various radio stations. Request Arbitron ratings from each station. Arbitron is a company that conducts private surveys to determine which groups listen to what radio station and when they listen. Arbitron periodically publishes these demographic statistics about the listeners for each station. By obtaining this information, you can most effectively determine the right station and time to place your commercial.

90

When selecting radio stations, choose the ones whose audience profiles your potential customer. Choosing the station that you listen to or the one that happens to be the least expensive is not necessarily your best buy. Also, there's no sense in paying a premium price to advertise on a station that covers four counties if you don't provide service to those areas—even if the station is the most popular.

I've found that running radio commercials during rush-hour traffic is the most effective time. You reach the working person who takes vacations, may travel on business and who presumably can afford your service.

Monday, Tuesday and Wednesday have been the best days to run my radio commercials. As with newspaper ads, the logic is that Thursday through Sunday are more popular vacation days, and your listening audience may not be as large. You want to reach the vacationers before they leave town.

TELEVISION—Some time ago I attended a workshop for small businesses. A local advertising executive spoke. After his presentation, I told him about my pet-sitting service and asked where I should put my advertising dollar. His emphatic reply was "television." I gasped, thinking *big money*, but he pointed out that families have pets, and families stay at home and watch television. Families also take vacations. He also noted that retired people and housewives watch daytime television, and working people watch morning news programs and night programming. In short, everyone watches television. According to him, the phenomenal number of people you can reach through television advertising makes it a bargain for your advertising dollar. So, with his advice in mind, I pursued advertising on a local TV station.

I quickly discovered that television advertising, indeed, is not cheap, but it is a lot more affordable than I had imagined. The station sales representative worked with me to tailor a commercial that would convey my message to the targeted viewing audience. Filming and starring in the commercial was an interesting and fun experience. I was both thrilled and proud when I saw the finished product for the first time in the studio. And when I saw my commercial on television, I felt my business had arrived.

Nevertheless, it was difficult to assess the effect of the television ads. Was the large expenditure worth the return? And what exactly was the return on my investment? It's hard to measure the effectiveness of radio and television commercials because of the nature of our product, pet-sitting services. In-home pet care is not something like food or cleaning products that are needed or used daily. A pet owner may see or listen to your commercial at Thanksgiving, but not need your services until the first week of July. Still, it was because of your radio or television commercial that he or she learned of your service.

Since the first edition of this book, I have conducted several marketing surveys to determine how clients heard about my pet-sitting service. Results of these surveys continue to indicate that the majority of our clients learned about us from three sources: (1) word-of-mouth referrals, (2) veterinarians and (3) newspaper advertising. Among the lowest-rated means of advertising were radio and television.

These surveys substantiate that the most expensive forms of advertising definitely are not the most effective for **my** pet-sitting service. Quite possibly, they won't prove to be most effective for **any** pet-sitting business. Considering the number of clients you have to gain to pay for a television commercial, I am now inclined to advise against using this method of advertising—unless you have a huge advertising budget or have tried everything else already. Instead, concentrate your efforts on doing a terrific job for your clients, so they will enthusiastically tell others about your services. After all, a word-of-mouth referral is generally considered to be the best means of advertising for any kind of business.

> *Note*: If you have a large advertising budget and do decide to use radio or television commercials, my experience has shown that ad prices are not etched in stone. Negotiate with your sales agent for the best possible price. Also, explore the cost of advertising on cable TV channels. You'll probably find these channels to be less expensive than the major network stations, and they often have a variety of flexible advertising packages available.

THE YELLOW PAGES—Advertising in the Yellow Pages of your local telephone directory is another way of reaching a mass audience. Although it is expensive for the small business, it's a necessary expenditure—especially when you're just getting started. This is because pet sitting is such a new service that many people aren't even aware of its existence. When making travel plans, they are likely to consult the Yellow Pages for boarding kennels in their area, but not for pet sitters. This is why you need an eye-catching ad that describes your alternative service.

In the past, pet sitters had little choice about the placement of our Yellow Page ads. We were automatically lumped under the heading of KENNELS or DOG AND CAT BOARDING, although neither accurately reflects the care we provide. This has not been all bad though. After all, with pet sitting still a new concept, many pet owners aren't aware of our personalized services and don't know to look for us, unless they see our listing with the more traditional, boarding or kennel option. With pet sitting growing and gaining in popularity, more telephone books offer the option of listing under SITTING SERVICES or PET SITTERS. It's a good idea, though, to remain under the traditional heading (or be listed under both) until you've established your name in the community.

During your first year or two of business, you need an enticing display ad, or at least something larger than the normal, free phone listing a business receives. You want to let the world know your service is available. After you've established a reputation, just your business name, number and perhaps a descriptive slogan in the Yellow Pages will suffice.

My initial experience with advertising in the Yellow Pages was not especially positive (perhaps clouded by an overly aggressive salesperson). But the results of my advertising surveys have shown that my Yellow Page ads are consistently among the top five methods of bringing in new customers. I consider the expense a necessary evil of doing business.

THE FAMILIAR IMAGE

In whatever advertising you do, continuity is important. Think of advertising campaigns for products or services you see every day. Surely the name of a local real estate company comes to your mind just from a glimpse of the design and company colors of its FOR

SALE signs posted throughout your community. You probably don't even need to read the signs. Remember, continuity and repeated exposure are crucial. So, it's a good idea to put thought, time and some dollars into a logo, slogan, company color(s) selection, brochure and ad design to promote your business. And then, get them out and keep them out for the public to see. You want your image to be so professional and your name so familiar that the public begins to think there's something wrong in not having a "personal pet sitter" from your organization.

> *Note*: Another bit of advice from my years of experience is that animals get noticed. If you want the public to notice, include animals in your advertising—whether it's a photograph, poster or television commercial.

DEVELOPING A NEWSLETTER

After you've been in business a while and have established a list of clients, you may want to consider sending a monthly, quarterly or semiannual newsletter to your customers. This is not only an effective means of advertising, it is also a public relations tool. A newsletter allows you to communicate with your clients and provide them with useful information, thereby lending credibility and sincerity to your business endeavors.

In each newsletter, I follow the same format. This practice saves both time and money because I don't have to create each newsletter anew. And it increases the recognition factor among my customers. They don't mistake the newsletter for junk mail.

First, as the business owner, I write a personal column to inform clients of any changes in our business or payment procedures. I also use this column to thank customers for using our services. Each newsletter includes informative material on the pet industry, pet care or pet-related organizations. And I introduce a couple of our pet sitters in each issue and usually add a pet-related cartoon or joke.

> *Note*: If you use any previously published material in your newsletter, make sure you obtain permission to do so. Plagiarism and copyright infringement are serious infractions of the law.

The newsletter should provide a service (useful information) to your clients. But you can and should use it to generate business as well. You can use it to announce special promotions, publish discount coupons, or even to place help-wanted ads. (Some of your customers may be interested in pet sitting or know someone else who is looking for part-time work.) I always keep extra copies of the current newsletter on hand. The newsletter and our brochure are mailed out to potential clients who request information about our services.

Printing a newsletter is relatively inexpensive. If you have a computer, you can print it yourself rather cheaply. But even having it done by a print shop is affordable. The largest expense will be your postage for mailing the newsletter. If you plan a frequent mailing schedule, you should consider obtaining a bulk-mail permit from your post office. The permit will greatly decrease your postage costs with mass mailings.

My clients indicate they genuinely appreciate receiving our newsletter. The pennies it costs to produce go a long way in showing our customers we appreciate them and are serious about pet sitting as a profession.

6

Examining
the Negatives

WHENEVER EXPLORING a possible investment or career opportunity, it is important to examine the negatives. I've been fortunate in experiencing very few serious problems in starting and operating a pet-sitting service, and the negative aspects have been far outweighed by the positive ones. I've found that most problems can be solved with a potent combination of common sense and determination. And many problems can be avoided or minimized with some forethought and preplanning.

Since the first edition of this book, many readers have asked me to address the drawbacks of pet sitting. Others have shared problems they've experienced or ones they've anticipated. This section is a combination of my experiences and those that readers have shared with me.

The biggest problem is faced mainly by pet sitters who work alone. If you don't have any employees, you may find yourself working nearly 365 days a year, since people travel year-round. Holidays are especially busy times for pet sitters, so you may find that family celebrations will have to be adjusted around your schedule. Of course, these problems can be remedied or minimized by having a staff of sitters; that way weekend and holiday assignments can be rotated. Or you can choose to operate your service only during certain months of the year, such as May to September. However, there are so many benefits to pet sitting that I've found the sacrifice of working on holidays to be a small concession.

> *Note*: If you plan to work alone, remember that a reputable pet sitter should have provisions for back-up services. This will allow you and your clients peace of mind should you, for whatever reason, not be able to personally fulfill visits as contracted.

Depending upon the area in which you live, weather can occasionally be a drawback to pet sitting. I'll be the first to admit that walking a dog (or several of them!) on a chilly, rainy day can be less than pleasurable, as is sliding around with a dog in six inches of sleet and snow. Still, I can't think of any job that comes without imperfections, can you? And when it's a gorgeous spring day and I'm out walking those same dogs, well, it's hard to believe that I actually get paid for having so much fun.

Burnout can also be a problem. While no profession is immune from it, a pet sitter (especially one that works alone) has to guard against it. Caring for pets can be so enjoyable that you may find yourself having a hard time telling clients "no" or "I'm already booked for next weekend." Not wanting to disappoint a client or lose out on the business, you'll find yourself taking on too much and running yourself ragged. Exhaustion soon leads to burnout. And, if you rarely have any time off, or continually miss out on holiday celebrations, you'll find burnout occurring sooner than later. But by recognizing that this threat exists, you'll be able to structure your staff accordingly, or schedule reservations wisely, to prevent burnout from ruining what can be a wonderful career.

A minor drawback to pet sitting is that you can expect to hear occasional criticism of your fees. When setting your prices, you'll probably find your fees are considerably higher than those of the local boarding kennel. Some pet owners are not accustomed to spending so much on their pet, whether it's for veterinary care, dietary needs or the tender, loving care you'll be providing. You just have to take this infrequent objection in stride and realize that you provide a specialized service that isn't going to be appreciated or utilized by everyone. Fortunately, many pet owners think the world of their pets and will gladly pay your fees, which are actually reasonable considering the peace of mind that your service allows them when they are away from home. My experience has been that for every person who complains that my fees are too high, there are probably five people who ask, "Is that all you charge?"

The last real disadvantage is something that every business faces eventually—plain old problems. These come in all shapes and sizes and seem to rear their ugly heads when we least need or want to deal with them. Problems that first come to mind about pet sitting are such things as: "What if I am bitten by a dog?" or "What if I lock myself out of a home?"

As I've mentioned before, most of the problems associated with pet sitting can be avoided by using common sense and doing your homework beforehand. Your homework should include reading the following question-and-answer section, as well as the rest of this book. You should also research and seek out other sources that will help you to intelligently and successfully operate your pet-sitting business. As with so many other things, an ounce of prevention is worth a pound of cure.

POSSIBLE PROBLEMS AND
HOW TO AVOID THEM

What if a pet I'm sitting for is hit by a car?

First of all, protect yourself by having a clause in your service contract that releases you from that liability if a pet you are sitting for has free access to the outdoors. Cats may disappear for days, and it's very possible they could be injured or killed, or they may disappear permanently. If you're going to care for these free spirits, make sure that you're protected with a signed release from liability.

Secondly, many areas have leash laws that prohibit dogs from running freely. Become familiar with leash laws and pet ordinances that apply to your community. As a reputable pet sitter, you would not want to risk violating such laws. Regardless of whether your area has a leash law, always walk a dog you're caring for on a leash. Point out to owners that they must provide you with a leash or allow you to supply your own; otherwise, you will not be able to sit for their pets.

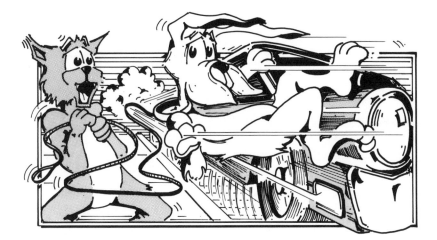

Thirdly, ask the client during your first meeting if the pet is notorious for trying to dash out of a door when someone enters, or if the pet has ever gotten loose on its own. Knowing this history beforehand will help you to prevent such problems from occurring.

By taking these precautions, you will greatly minimize the chances a pet will be hit by a car, or your liability if such an accident should occur.

How do I make sure a pet I'm sitting for doesn't run away or get lost?

Be sure and ask clients who have fenced areas for their pets if the enclosed area is secure. Often, dogs will have a favorite spot they dig at, trying to escape. You'll need to know where to look for this spot and how to remedy the situation. And, with the theft of pets being an ongoing concern, you may want to require that all outdoor gates to pet areas be securely locked during the owner's absence. A locked gate will keep neighborhood children away from the pet as well.

It's a smart idea to require that pets be current on all vaccinations and that they wear a collar with identification if they spend any time out of doors. You should also make notes on your service contract, identifying the breed, sex and age of the pet(s). This information may be helpful in identifying a pet or obtaining medical care, if necessary, while the owner is away.

What if a repairman shows up at a client's home while I'm caring for a pet?

Never let anyone into a client's home unless you have been specifically authorized (in writing on your service contract) to do so by the client. And then, do so only after the visitor has presented you with satisfactory identification. Even if it's the next-door neighbor wanting to borrow a cup of sugar, you can be liable. You may have to replace a broken sugar bowl if the neighbor breaks it. In such a case, you might decide to lend the sugar if the neighbor provides something to put it in, but you should get the sugar yourself. Don't let even a neighbor into a client's house.

100

What if a client complains that I forgot to water the plants, as requested?

This is why your service contract is very important. Get all your instructions in writing. It is preferable, by the way, to let the client fill out the contract form. When the client has completed the form, review it carefully (making sure you can read the handwriting) and add any notations to yourself. By having the client complete the form, you ensure that your job responsibilities are clearly spelled out. Then, if the plants aren't watered, it won't be because you forgot, but because the client failed to ask you to do so. A conscientious pet sitter will notice a room filled with plants and ask the homeowner if they need to be watered. If plants need this care, he or she will note this in the service contract.

What if a toilet overflows when I try to flush the cat litter?

Try to get specific instructions from the client about how to dispose of the litter. Never flush the litter unless your client has instructed you in writing to do so. If you are expected to dispose of it in the toilet, ask where the plumber's helper is stored, in the event of a clogged drain. If a toilet does overflow, don't continue to use it. Instead, dispose of the litter in plastic bags to be placed in the outside garbage can.

What if I'm late in getting to a client's home to feed and care for the pet(s)?

This should not happen often because your dependability is basic to your reputation. However, if you find yourself delayed due to car problems, traffic jams or mischievous critters at another customer's home, use your daily note to tell your client why you were late. Then, do your best to make sure your next visits are more prompt. Honesty is always the best policy. Just as sure as you don't explain that you were late one morning, a watchful neighbor will inform your client of the fact, and you can expect a complaint.

What if I notice a urine stain on the carpet?

Always ask your clients how pet accidents should be cleaned in their homes. Even if the client swears the pet is house-trained and that accidents will not occur, get cleaning instructions just in case. Pets often behave differently when their owners are absent, and a change in these habits is typically how pets express their loneliness or anger. If you live in an area where inclement weather sometimes precludes service rounds from being safely made, you can expect some puddles and messes that will need to be cleaned up.

How do I handle a pet sitter who tries to sell my clients other services having nothing to do with my business?

As you increase your staff, you will probably find many of your sitters have other jobs. It's important to instruct your sitters that while they are performing their pet-sitting duties, pet sitting should be their primary concern. Sitters should not approach customers for self-serving reasons while they are working for you. When a sitter goes to meet a pet owner, he or she should present your company's business card and talk pets—not real estate or homemade crafts. If the sitter acts more interested in recruiting a client's real estate business than the pet care at hand, the integrity of your service is diminished in the mind of the customer.

What should I do about clients who return home earlier than anticipated but don't call to discontinue my services?

This lack of consideration causes pet sitters unnecessary trips, and I know of some sitters who have found themselves in embarrassing situations as a result. (One of my sitters arrived at the customer's home for a scheduled 6:45 a.m. visit only to walk in on the client in his underwear in the kitchen making coffee! Needless to say, this was a startling and awkward situation for both parties. . . . The client now calls immediately if he returns home sooner than expected.)

To protect and compensate yourself for these unnecessary trips, have a policy in writing, either in your company's brochure or service contract, covering this situation. My inclination is to hit the client where it hurts (in the pocketbook) and charge full price for any wasted trips due to his or her negligence. This is reasonable for your time, travel and inconvenience and may prompt a client to remember to call you upon return the next time.

What do I say to clients who request late night visits for their pets or who want additional services I don't generally perform?

As to the late night visits, that is up to you. It is a company policy that needs to be determined in advance and strictly adhered to. Because the majority of my sitters are women and there's a greater risk of danger for them late at night, I do not offer late night visits to pets. I simply explain this policy to clients, and they have always understood from a liability standpoint. I would much rather clean up pet messes the next morning than risk something happening to one of my staff members. There have been only a couple of exceptions to this rule through the years. They were both cases in which the pet required medication at several times of the day, and the client was a long-standing customer. We made the visits but charged extra for doing so. Both clients were happy to pay the additional charge and realized that we were bending the rules in order to accommodate their pets' special needs.

As to providing additional services, this too is something you'll need to consider in advance. If you're willing to comply with special requests, either have an hourly rate established for your help or a per-task fee in mind. If time or liability constraints dictate that you stick strictly to pet-sitting chores, then simply explain this to your clients. This is why they called you in the first place, and they should understand that you aren't a jack of all trades.

What do I do if a teenager or college student appears at one of the homes I'm sitting for and tells me he or she will take over care of the pets?

Never take anyone's word for anything around the home except the person who hired you and signed your contract authorizing services. This person is your employer and the one responsible for your bill. I've heard of too many stories of teenagers or college students who are supposed to be at school or staying with someone. Instead, they sneak home to throw a big party while Mom and Dad are away. . . . This scenario spells trouble with the liability at hand. So, tell the young person that you'll need to use their phone to call the parents and verify this fact. And then **do** speak with the client before ceasing any services.

How do I prevent clients from calling their assigned sitter at home rather than making reservations through our office as they should?

First, stress to all your sitters the importance in having all reservations made through your office. Point out how it could damage your company's reputation if a client calls only the sitter and leaves a message on an answering machine that services are needed starting immediately. What if the sitter is on vacation or otherwise unavailable? The message would not be received, yet the client would leave assuming service would be provided. Since your office personnel should know which sitters are available and which are not during any time period, all reservations need to come through the proper channel.

When a sitter understands all this, he or she can tactfully

explain the rationale for your policy that clients must go through the office for reservations. Should a client persist in calling the sitter directly, you'll need to call the customer or write a letter that firmly requests cooperation in this matter. If a client still doesn't comply, then discontinue providing sitting services to this individual.

Another reason you'll want all reservations coming through your office is if you provide liability insurance and a dishonesty bond. For this you'll need an accurate record of all sitting assignments undertaken by your company. If you have no documentation of the job, your insurance company may deny coverage on any claim related to it.

And speaking of insurance, it is vital. You must protect yourself: a pet may be lost or injured while under your care; personal property in a pet owner's home could be damaged or stolen; or other equally unsavory things might occur. One uninsured incident could not only ruin your business but your reputation as well. After clients hear that your insurance may not cover them unless reservations are made through your office, they're usually only too happy to request services this way.

7

Useful
Business Forms

PROFESSIONAL, EFFECTIVE business forms are extremely important to any reputable pet-sitting service. A well-thought-out form can save you valuable time, streamline your company procedures, protect your assets and enhance your company's image. You'll be wise to devote your attention, energies and money to developing forms that will best benefit your service.

In this chapter, I will give you an overview of the forms most highly recommended for a pet sitter and discuss some of their necessary ingredients. Since a service contract will probably be your most important document, let's begin our discussion with it.

DESIGNING A SERVICE CONTRACT

You will use this form to gather information about each assignment and it will also serve as your legal agreement to perform pet-sitting services for a client on his or her premises. I highly recommend that you consult with an attorney before using any contract you have written to ensure that it adequately protects you. Still, the following advice should help you prepare a rough draft or mock-up to review with your attorney.

Client Information

First, the service contract can be divided into sections. The first section allows you to gather information about the client. You'll need spaces for the client's name, address, home and business phone numbers. You'll want to know the date that the customer is leaving town and when he or she anticipates returning. And there should be room for the client to write where he or she can be reached (address and telephone number). You'll also be wise to find out the name of a local friend, family member or neighbor to contact in the event of an emergency—should you be unable to reach the client. After all, people on vacation do not sit in their rooms waiting for their pet sitter to call. If a home under your care is burglarized, the pet sitter probably won't know about valuables in the home that may be missing, something law enforcement officers would need to know. Having a close friend or family member to call on may help in such a situation.

Other Keys

You'll also want to list on your service contract who else has a key to the home. This list can be part of the first section. There are several reasons why this is important. If the home is burglarized, the pet sitter will be able to provide the police with a list of key holders, which would aid in the investigation. Also, occasionally a client will have his or her home for sale without displaying a FOR SALE sign. The sitter may arrive to care for a pet and find a real estate agent and family of four walking through the home. Hopefully, reading this question on your service contract will remind the client to inform the sitter that a real estate agent has a housekey. And, finally, should a pet sitter do the unthinkable and lock herself out of the house, it's nice to know the neighbor three doors away also has a key.

Natural Circumstances

If you live in an area of inclement weather or natural disasters such as earthquakes or hurricanes, you should also have a written PLAN B of action on your contract. Natural circumstances beyond our control may make it hazardous or impossible to make our pet-sitting visits. Having the name and number of a client's nearby neighbor may be a crucial part of PLAN B.

Pet Information

The next portion of your contract should deal with the information you'll need to have about the pets. There are several things you'll want to include on your service contract: the pet's name, type, breed, sex, age, diet, medication and exercise requirements. Leave enough room so that you can make notations to yourself, such as "Taffy is the white cat and Samantha is the Siamese." It's important to have good notations; if you're sitting for several different clients on the same days, it may be easy to get instructions or pets confused.

It's also wise to obtain the pet's medical history on your service contract. The little Chihuahua having seizures on your morning visit

will throw you into a panic, unless you know this is normal for the dog and that rushing it to the vet isn't necessary.

But should the seizures NOT be normal, you'll also want to have the client's veterinarian's name and telephone number at hand. You should also obtain permission from the client to seek medical attention for his or her pet.

Something you may not think of asking is where the client stores the pet food. Not everyone keeps it in the same place, and I've found it stored in pantries, garage trash cans and bathroom closets. It's been in containers on top of a refrigerator. Rarely is it stored in what you may consider to be a logical place. Save yourself time and a potential problem by learning this in advance.

You'll also want to know if the pet is allowed treats. Many four-legged creatures count their calories these days, and you don't want to sabotage any diets by offering treats.

Last, but certainly not least, ask if the pet has any favorite forms of affection or exercise. If it loves to have its ears scratched or to chase a Frisbee, you want to know in order to make the most of the special time you'll be spending with the pet. Find out what you can do to make the pet feel loved and happy during the owner's absence. It's this personalized part of our service that makes it so unique and appealing, and it's why the client most likely called you in the first place. Make sure that you deliver lots of Tender Loving Care.

Household Routines

The third section of your service contract should address pertinent information regarding the client's home. Spell out any additional household services you're willing to provide and the extra fee for each chore. Then, you or the client can simply check off what he or she would like done—the newspaper and mail brought inside, the lights alternated, the plants watered, etc.

You may want to ask if the client would like the radio or television left on during his or her absence. This is a good crime deterrent, as it provides noise and the impression of activity inside the home. It also provides companionship for some pets.

It's a good idea to ask if the client would like his or her telephone answered. This was something I had not anticipated when I first began pet sitting. I found it was a strange feeling to be in someone's home and hear the phone ring and ring. I suppose it's almost a natural reflex or habit to want to answer a ringing phone! Shortly after this experience, there was an article in my local newspaper about a theft ring that had recently been caught in the act. The thieves had been calling homes and, if there was no answer, they would go to the home. If the phone was still ringing when they arrived, they knew no one was there and would break into the home. Learning about this ingenious little scheme was all I needed to begin asking my customers if they would like their telephone answered. Some customers feel that it's not necessary, while others appreciate the attention to detail this offer shows. When I am expected to answer the phone, I always act as if I am a full-time housesitter staying in the home while the owner is away. Should the caller be someone unscrupulous, hopefully, this will prevent any wrongdoing. To date, though, it has always been a friendly voice on the other end of the telephone line. Of course, I always leave the customer a message with the caller's name and number, as well as the date and time of the call.

> *Note*: With the popularity of answering machines today, a client may tell you just to let his or her machine take care of all calls. It's wise to ask the customer if he or she will be checking messages during this absence from home. If the answer is yes, and you need to let the client know something that's not quite important enough for a long-distance call, you can leave a message on the answering machine. An example might be: "This is Jane, your XYZ Pet Sitter. Just wanted to let you know that we had an unexpected snowfall last night with about eight inches accumulation. Due to the record cold temperatures and snow, I brought your dogs into the basement to weather out the evening more comfortably. If there's any problem with leaving them inside during the evenings until it warms up some, please call me at my home number 999–2403. Thank you."

Extra Services

You should also allow enough space in the third section of your service contract for notes about any extra services that may be requested. These will be tasks above and beyond your normal responsibilities, and if you're willing to perform them, you will need to negotiate fees while meeting with the client. Examples that come to mind from my own experience include watering a client's greenhouse full of plants. Although my service normally allows for the watering of a few household plants, this particular client, an avid horticulturist, was asking for more. While I was happy to be able to help her by looking after the greenhouse, I did have to charge a considerable amount for the extra time. (I also had her sign a statement that said I would not be liable if any of her plants died, as I am truly not a green thumb!)

Another client inquired if his dry cleaning could be picked up. And one family, which would be returning late at night after a three-week trip to Europe, asked if some breakfast groceries could be left in their refrigerator. One of the funniest requests was to "feed the bread." Making sourdough bread requires keeping a starter base in the refrigerator and "feeding" it every few days with a couple of ingredients such as potato flakes. This particular client said she felt like an idiot making the request but, needless to say, she was relieved and thrilled to learn I'd do this for her while looking after her Poodles. It only took a minute or two to add the ingredients, so I didn't even charge her extra. On my first visit to her home while she was away, a freshly baked loaf of this wonderful bread was on her kitchen table! Sometimes it pays to be nice. When discussing extras with clients, keep in mind that most people know if their requests are beyond the scope of your normal services. Usually they are more than happy to pay extra for special requests. So, don't let a customer try to take advantage of you; this, fortunately, probably won't be attempted very often.

Returning Housekeys

How a customer's housekey is to be returned should also be clarified on your service contract. Returning a key personally may be the preferable way, as it gives you and the client peace of mind in knowing the key got to the rightful owner. This visit also prompts the customer to pay you for your services at that time and often will get you a tip as well. However, it does take additional time and travel to return a housekey, so make sure your pet-sitting fees can absorb these costs, or consider charging a nominal amount for key return. As noted in an earlier chapter, many homes these days have deadbolt locks that require a key to lock them. Thus, these keys have to be personally returned anyway.

> *Note*: Beware of the client (one without deadbolt locks) who instructs you to leave the key on the kitchen counter and lock yourself out of the home after your final visit. This would be fine except that flights are missed or delayed, cars break down and inclement weather may make it impossible for the owner to return when anticipated. If the key has been locked inside the home, an expensive locksmith will be necessary for you to continue caring for the pets and home. A word to the wise: Agree to leave the key well hidden outside for the client if he or she does not want it personally returned. In this way, you still have access to the home, should it be necessary.

Of course there will be many clients who just adore your service and use it frequently. They will eventually request that you simply retain a key until further notice. This gesture of trust speaks well for your services and saves you time and travel. And, don't be surprised one day to receive a call from one of these clients who has inadvertently locked himself out of the house and needs you to come to his rescue with your key. Yes, a professional pet sitter can be a godsend in more ways than one! But remember, retaining housekeys permanently increases your liability. Discuss this aspect with your insurance agent and attorney and do be sure to safeguard client's keys at all times.

Fees and Hours

It's important to have your established fees and normal route hours listed on your service contract, so everything is clearly spelled out. However, some pet sitters prefer to have a separate fee schedule as an addendum to their business literature. The rationale is that if fees change, the whole service contract does not have to be reprinted. Regardless of the procedure you choose, make sure there is a place on your contract to fill in what the client's total fee will be. This should be understood and agreed to before your services begin.

You should also consider noting on your service contract whether any type of cancellation fee applies and under what circumstances. If something prevents a customer's trip from taking place, you still have to consider the time and travel pet sitters have invested in initial interviews, as well as the fact that your service was planning on this job as a source of revenue.

Another policy that may be important to list on your service contract is whether or not you have a one-time only visit charge. An example of this would be the client who is going to a nearby town for a football game. He expects to return home later on that same day and only needs one suppertime visit made to feed and exercise his dog. Unless your fee is a bit higher for these types of visits, they're probably not worth the time and effort of initial interviews and returning housekeys.

Legal Considerations

The last part of a service contract should also contain the "legalese" that will explain exactly who is responsible for what regarding terms and conditions of this agreement. Making sure that your service contract adequately protects you and makes your client feel comfortable as well is a delicate matter; it probably requires the advice and direction of an attorney. You want to be absolutely sure that your service contract will be a binding agreement.

When meeting with your attorney to draw up the contract, consider addressing questions such as:

1) When and how must the customer pay for rendered services?
2) Who is responsible for veterinarians' fees if such assistance becomes necessary during the owner's absence?
3) Who is responsible for extra time expended by a pet sitter due to emergencies regarding the pet or home?
4) Who is responsible for purchases—such as additional cat litter or paper towels—necessary for the satisfactory performance of duties?
5) Under what, if any, circumstances can you or your company be held liable during the duration of the contract?

6) Under what, if any, circumstances will the client be held liable during the duration of the contract?

7) When do the terms of the contract actually begin and end?

8) If other people will have access to the home at the same time you do, will the client release you from liability for any damage that could result from the other parties' negligence?

As you can see from the implications these questions bring to mind, having a well-thought-out service contract is extremely important. While structuring this part of your form may seem overwhelming, don't let it frighten you or prevent you from getting into the wonderful world of pet sitting. Just take your time, think through all of these points, hash them out with objective friends or family members, then visit a good attorney for his or her advice and appropriate direction. Consider your creation of a thorough and professional service contract to be a one-time investment that will guide you well in the years to come.

> *Note*: The legally binding aspects of a service contract are the signatures of the parties involved. So be sure that your service contract has a signature line for the client and pet sitter and a place for the date that the contract was entered into. And by all means, make sure that you obtain the client's signature on this critical document!

INVOICE

Some pet sitters give the client a copy of the service contract that lists the total amount due, and this serves as the customer's invoice. This procedure cuts down on accounting and postage costs. However, some clients don't realize that the service contract is their invoice, and they often have to be reminded of the payment procedure several times.

Other pet sitters have a separate invoice that they use for billing. Some design this form themselves and have it preprinted with their company name, address and logo, while others purchase a basic invoice from an office supply store and personalize it with a rubber stamp.

Whichever method you choose for your business, an invoice is a fairly basic and simple form. It usually includes an invoice number, what the bill is for and when payment is due. Although not necessary, it's a nice gesture to include a self-addressed envelope with the invoice for the customer's convenience when paying.

DAILY LOG

As stated earlier, it's my opinion that every professional and reputable pet-sitting service needs some kind of daily log form. Some pet sitters simply use a scratch pad for writing the daily report for the client. Others have professionally printed forms for these notes. Other pet sitters use a checklist and mark off daily tasks as they are completed. Notations may be made at the bottom of this form, should the pet sitter observe anything that may be of interest to the client.

Your own ideas and creativity may lead you to design a totally different type of daily log to meet the needs of your pet-sitting service. In any event, I encourage you to have some kind of daily log an integral part of your service.

EVALUATION FORM

The value of this type of form to you as a business owner is immeasurable. It allows clients the chance to give you feedback that will keep your services on target and progressive. A well-designed evaluation form will help you assess what aspects of your services are well received and who is doing the best job in delivering those services. After all, if you have a staff of pet sitters, they most likely work independently without direct supervision. You need some way of knowing the job they are doing as representatives of your company. An evaluation form will provide this information.

Although some clients will not take the time to fill out and return such a form, many of them will be impressed and complimented that their opinion matters and will eagerly respond. My own clients have been very helpful in returning this form, and some have made suggestions that have improved our services.

I know of some pet sitters who leave a report card type of evaluation that allows the client to grade the sitter's performance and note the customer's degree of satisfaction with services rendered. Others go into more detail, asking the client specific questions such as "Did the pet sitter arrive on time?" "Was the pet sitter conscientious and caring?" and "Were your instructions followed?"

Another extremely important function of this form is that it permits you to ask clients how they first heard about your pet-sitting service. These replies can clue you in to what advertising is bringing you results. And with the high cost of advertising, you do want to know where you're getting the most for your buck.

I insist that my pet sitters leave a self-addressed evaluation form on their last visit to a customer's home. The recourse this form allows our clients gives them a comfortable feeling about the professionalism of our service. And, should a client not return an evaluation form, it's a good idea to follow up with a telephone call to ascertain that the client was pleased with your services.

ADDITIONAL FORMS

The forms already discussed are probably the most basic for use by a reputable pet sitter just starting out. However, as you discuss liabilities with your insurance agent and attorney, there may be strong arguments for the development of other pertinent business forms. For example, one sitting service I know has all clients fill out and sign a form that dictates their wishes in the event of their pet's death during the sitting assignment. Another has a separate form that pertains to the safekeeping and liabilities associated with the client's housekey. A third service has a more detailed form that deals with the health history and habits of each pet. While some forms—such as a client information card, service contract and brochure—are found in all pet-sitting businesses, others are developed to meet the personal needs of each service.

And of course, as your business grows, you'll need such things as employment application forms. Standard employment applications can be purchased in most office supply stores, but they are rudimentary in nature. With the unique demands of pet sitting, a more comprehensive employment application is required to help you determine which candidates are best suited for your openings. With time, you'll soon know the questions to ask job applicants and will be able to design your own application or alter a store-bought form accordingly.

Note: To avoid violating any state or federal hiring laws, it's advisable to consult with an attorney about any employment application you use in your business.

8

In Conclusion

TRACKING YOUR GROWTH

You may find it helpful to chart such details as the number of daily inquiries received about your service or the number of reservations or assignments per month, per holiday, per zip code, etc. This can be charted by making checkmarks on a calendar or keeping a log of customer names by various categories. There will be a discouraging day every now and then, and it's reassuring to refer to these sheets to see how you've grown since last Easter or Labor Day.

Keeping these types of records will also help you to learn the busiest areas and times for your business. Knowing this will assist you in staffing appropriately and scheduling the best time for your own vacation.

BUSINESS TRENDS

Although my business has grown to the point that it now remains fairly steady, slow periods do occur and are to be expected. Fortunately, my pet-sitting service is located in a city that is only a couple of hours away from the coast to the east and the mountains to the west. These close vacation spots provide me with winter business from skiers, as well as year-round business from area beach buffs.

I've found my busiest season begins with Easter and continues through Labor Day. This is the traditional family vacation period and has the nicest weather. September and October are both good months for us due to many clients who go on fall fishing trips, foliage tours and those who prefer to vacation when the kids are back in school. November keeps us busy with the Thanksgiving vacation period, and Christmas is absolutely the busiest holiday of all. The slower months are January, February and March, which is probably due to people rebounding from holiday spending, computing their taxes owed or just plain nesting due to bad weather. I like to use the slower months to recuperate from the busy season and clean files and catch up on busywork. And I also try to get away to some warm, sunny destination!

My experience has shown that people travel for many reasons: business, pleasure and often because of family emergencies. Some people prefer a January vacation, while others always vacation the third week of July. There is no rule of thumb for when people travel. The good side to this is you'll find your pet-sitting services needed throughout the year. The downside to this is that there's no way to predict or guage the amount of business you'll do each month, and this at times can be frustrating.

Don't be surprised to find your services in demand even when the client is not leaving home. Sometimes pet owners will need your help due to an illness or injury that prevents them from properly caring for their pets. Other times, long working hours may prompt a pet owner to request your services. And some dog owners, kept busy at work, will want a monthly contract with you to walk and exercise their pooches at lunchtime each day. It's a good idea to advertise your services as useful for the ''in-town'' pet owner, as well as to those who must travel. This may increase your volume of business.

SOME CLOSING THOUGHTS

Every successful endeavor begins with one small step. By purchasing and reading this book, you've taken that first small step toward opening your own successful business.

Pet sitting has provided me with an enjoyable, challenging and rewarding career. As mentioned at the beginning of this book, when I began pet sitting there was little information available to guide me. I've had to work long and hard to develop my successful business and elevate pet sitting to a recognized, respectable and credible profession. The demand for in-home pet care has just recently begun to sweep the country, and this trend has made pet sitting an up-and-coming career.

It's now up to you. Pet sitting is an exciting, interesting, fun business that requires a relatively low up-front investment. The need for this service exists in large and small communities, and it can be met with your sincere and energetic commitment to provide the best in personalized home pet care. Remember that the pioneers in this field are counting on you to uphold and continue the standards of excellence that are necessary for successful pet sitters. Hopefully, this book will make meeting this requirement much easier for future pet sitters everywhere.

Addenda

HELPFUL PRODUCTS FOR PROFESSIONAL PET SITTERS

As stated at the outset, much of what I have learned about the pet-sitting business has been through trial and error. It has been my intent, in writing this book, to save other prospective pet sitters some of the hassle, headaches and money that I went through in establishing and successfully operating my own business. Along the way, there have been some ideas, methods and products that I've found extremely beneficial. In a continuing effort to help other pet sitters and improve the standards of the pet-sitting industry, I've made many of these items available at reasonable prices through my company Patti Moran's Products for Professional Pet Sitters. A list of these products follows. They're all tried and true products that will assist you in efficiently, economically and professionally operating your pet-sitting business. I encourage you to write for additional information.

Professional Pet Sitting Starter Kits Allow you to start pet sitting professionally easily and economically. Available in Essential, Entrepreneur and Executive versions to meet your career goals.

The New Pet Sitter Forty-five minute orientation video covers day-to-day basics of responsible pet-sitting care. An all-inclusive resource that comes with a pop quiz. A valuable training aid that allows you to professionally train AND test staff members.

Business Forms for Pet-Sitting Professionals. These forms save you valuable time and streamline your office procedures while enhancing your company's image. Everything from the all-important service contract to employment applications is available. Each camera-ready form may be reprinted by your local printer.

"What IS Pet Sitting?" Video This seven-minute video describes the benefits of leaving a pet at home and explains how most professional pet-sitting services operate. A terrific public relations aid, this video will enhance your guest speaking engagements and impress viewers with the professionalism of the pet-sitting industry.

PZZZ . . . Ads Advertisement Campaign A successful, market-tested ad campaign that brings your service increased revenues and name recognition, while bringing a smile to your customers' faces. Seasonal, holiday and year-round ads. Camera-ready material.

"PAWSITIVELY PROUD" Professional Pet Sitter Apparel T-shirts, sweatshirts, sweatpants, shorts, and even "Bad Hair Day" caps for pet sitters. Comfortable and color-coordinated, this casual attire allows you to look neat, remain comfortable, and be prepared for muddy paws!

PET-SIT II A software application program specifically designed for pet-sitting companies. To be used with the versatile PROFESSIONAL FILE software program. Helps you take control of your business and manage it more productively.

> and there's more . . . For ordering information on these and our other products, please write or call:
>
> Patti Moran's Products for Professional Pet Sitters
> 540 High Bridge Road, Dept. H
> Pinnacle, NC 27043
> (910) 983-2444 1:30–5:00 p.m. EST
> (910) 983-3755 FAX

PET SITTERS INTERNATIONAL

Pet Sitters International (PSI) is an organization which I began for professional pet sitters who are interested in improving and promoting the at-home pet care industry. Through affiliation with PSI, members enjoy networking with other pet-sitting professionals and staying informed on industry practices and concerns through our quarterly publication, "The Professional Pet Sitter."

Pet Sitters International also makes available a low cost liability insurance program to members in the USA. This coverage was designed exclusively for the professional pet sitter and takes the worry and the hassle out of finding reliable coverage. Best of all, buying this protection through PSI membership means affordable group rates.

Other benefits of PSI membership include discounts and special rates on services and products that are important to the success of the professional pet sitter. Plus, PSI provides publicity-generating materials and media referrals which can help to build your business.

Based on my own experiences as a professional pet sitter, as founder of the National Association of Pet Sitters, and on feedback from numerous colleagues, I've created Pet Sitters International to give professional pet sitters the membership benefits you want and need most. And, membership is priced at a fee which is well within the budget of even the smallest pet-sitting service.

If you're serious about your pet-sitting career, I urge you to join Pet Sitters International. Membership will keep your education ongoing in this new industry and help you to be your professional best!

For more information please contact:

Pet Sitters International
418 East King Street
King, NC 27021
(910) 983-9222
(910) 983-3755 FAX

ESTIMATED START-UP COSTS AND CHECKLIST

Business License(s) .... _____

Name Registration .... _____

Attorney .... _____

Legal Structure .... _____

    (partnership agreement, incorporation, etc.)

Bond and Insurance Coverages .... _____

Accounting Assistance and Advice .... _____

Rent for Office Space .... _____

Deposit for Office Space .... _____

Moving Expenses for Set-Up of Office Site .... _____

Business Telephone Installation .... _____

Business Telephone Deposit .... _____

Monthly Charge for Business Telephone .... _____

Telephone (Purchase or Rental) .... _____

Answering Machine or .... _____

Personal Answering Service .... _____

Calculator .... _____

Typewriter or .... _____

Computer and Software .... _____

Desk .... _____

Chair .... _____

File Cabinet .... _____

Shelf or Bookcase .... _____

Advertising

    Newspaper .... _____

    Local publications .... _____

    Radio .... _____

Television .... _____

Yellow Pages .... _____

Other .... _____

.... _____

Professional Affiliations and Subscriptions

Annual Dues for:

    Pet-Related Organizations .... _____

    Chamber of Commerce .... _____

    Better Business Bureau .... _____

    National Association of Pet Sitters .... _____

Reference Books

    Business-related .... _____

    Pet-related .... _____

    Other .... _____

Magazine Subscriptions

    Business-related .... _____

    Pet-related .... _____

    Other .... _____

POSTSCRIPT

Several years ago my husband and I purchased a travel book before taking a trip through Europe. We found the book especially helpful, not only for information the author supplied, but also for the tips and suggestions readers had provided from their European travels. I would like to provide this same kind of firsthand experience from readers when this book is revised and reissued. Please write to me of things you find helpful and successful in your pet-sitting service, and I'll try to incorporate them in future editions.

Patti J. Moran
New Beginnings
540 High Bridge Road, Dept. H
Pinnacle, NC 27043

It's a big world out there with lots of room for successful pet-sitting services. Let's help ourselves, our colleagues and our industry to be the best that they can be. Please know that I wish you good luck and good fortune with your pet-sitting business.